Wealth To Self Development

OrangeBooks Publication

1st Floor, Rajhans Arcade, Mall Road, Kohka, Bhilai, Chhattisgarh 490020

Website: **www.orangebooks.in**

© Copyright, 2024, Author

All rights reserved. No part of this book may be reproduced, stored in a retrieval system, or transmitted, in any form by any means, electronic, mechanical, magnetic, optical, chemical, manual, photocopying, recording or otherwise, without the prior written consent of its writer.

First Edition, 2024

ISBN: 978-93-5621-854-3

Wealth To Self Development

A path to new dimension of life

SHOBHANA

OrangeBooks Publication
www.orangebooks.in

Put everything together and grab your hands to build the life of temple where your consciousness and awareness is the real God & Goddess, ready to bless & protect you.

Author's Preface

How to start? What to start? Everything started from an unknown thing. Yes, it is a surprise that I am writing a book and all of sudden became an author. A yearlong beautiful journey with lots of learning perceived, as I wrote this book. I very proudly announce this book **"WEALTH TO SELF DEVELOPMENT"** is fully based upon writer's previous life journey. It had been a hard-earned journey which is now transformed into a book of wisdom.

This book has come to me by God's will since I never dreamt to be an author. But this book surely will change the perspective of life we have been living so far. Even though I am a first-time author, I believe this book will change each one of the lives of the people who are reading it. I know this book is going to create magic in everybody's life.

This book has different chapters which encapsulate each and every stage, behaviour and emotions of life. It is a book that will briefly explain how human life has to be led, followed and be liberated (enlightened) in order to reach your higher self. I believe this book will surely bring wisdom in each one's life because it personally has taught me a lot about how I should live hereafter and what is my purpose on this earthly plane, born as this particular being.

Dear readers, miracles always happen in life and I am one of the living proofs, here presenting this book for you. Everything happened just like that, how a normal human being can get the power to write such a beautiful, spiritual book making everything understandable for a common layman.

It is the power of higher consciousness to bless me and bring me to this stage of life. Everyone is looking for God's blessings. But I am the luckiest to be blessed for being a blessing to myself.

I believe this book will change your consciousness and awareness even before you finish reading this book.

Acknowledgements

Thank you God, for all the blessings and love you have showered on me to write this book. Thank you to my dear guru, **"Srimath Mahan Mounaguru Reddy Swamigal,"** for your blessings and support, without you this book would not have been possible. Thank you to one and all who stood behind as support to release this book. Thank you, universal higher consciousness for guiding and supporting me.

Contents

Part 1

Generalising Yourself With Life (To Live)

Thank You	1
Compassionate	5
Courage	8
Strength	11
Love	15
Divinity	18
Friendship	22
Self-Discipline	25
Happiness	28
Positive Thinking	30
Evaluate	33
Respect	36
Delightful	38
Appreciate	40
Relationship	43
Forgiveness	46

Attitude	49
Simplicity	52
Focus	54
Character	57
Purpose	60
Sympathy	63
Pleasure	65
Beautify	68
Aspiration	71
Patience	74
Sacrifice	77
Judgemental	80
Accomplishment	83
Unimaginable	86
Limitless	89
Impossible	92
Self-Esteem	95
Embarrassing	98
Silence	101
Possessiveness	104
Prejudice	107
Enthusiasm	110
Empowerment	113

Greatness 116

Certainty 119

Unsuccessful 121

Powerfulness 124

Uniqueness 127

Divineness 130

Faithfulness 133

Blissfulness 136

Richness 140

Believing 143

Part 2

Depth Of Knowledge To Live (To Know)

Being Supernatural 147

The Interlink 151

Universal Dimensions 154

Unconditional Love 159

Question Yourself 163

Reincarnation 167

Undeveloped Thoughts 171

The Indefinite Layers 174

Electrify Yourself 177

Layers Of Life 180

Traditional Career	183
Shield Yourself	188
Times Up	191
Taking Help	195
Be Wise	198
Be Alive	201
The Sword	204
Trust Yourself	208

Part 3

**How Are You Finishing Yourself?
(To Understand)**

The Untold Story Of You	212
Willingness To Live The Life You Want To Live	225
Happy To Live This Life?	229
You Have Been Teleported	232
You Are A Treasure Box	235
Are You Tolerating At Your Heart Level?	238
Great Value Of Life	241
Jurisdiction Of Your Life	245
Mistakes Of Life	248
Making Of The Universe	251
Development Of Thoughts	254
How Are You Willing To Live This Life?	257

You Are Destined 260
New Life Time Process 263
The Definition Of Life 266
Biochemistry Of Your Life 269
Are You Doubting Yourself? 273
Benefits Of Being Human 276
Respect To Yourself 279

Letter To My Guru 282
My Point Of View On My Life 287
What Questions You Have, Ask Me 290
Conclusion 299

Part 1

Generalising Yourself With Life (To Live)

Thank You

"Grow up the Thank you nature to nurture your life of success very easily and carry the happiness of success with the words of Thank you, Thank you".

The word **"Thank you"** is so precisely defined to mention the love you have for the things that you have for yourself.

"Thank you" is a gratitude note that acknowledges the multitude of things that surround you. It feels the rise of appreciation and kindness in accordance with sources you carry. Great things just happen as miracles within a few minutes of time, not consuming anything from you.

"Thank you" is the ultimate word to start anything or to end anything. If you need gross benefit from everything in life, just say "Thank you" in each and every part of life moment. Moving and growing with gratitude is the greatest blessing that a human can receive in this life. Go to every end of life that makes you feel special, only by working on the word "Thank you".

The call of gratitude towards your life is such a great blessing that is unearthed from the bottom of your heart. Carry on with each and every moment of your life in happiness of gratitude to feel the love you have for life.

"Cooperate yourself in each and every moment in such a way that all the favours of life are always meant for you".

You copy each moment of life to take care of gratitude in such a way that it keeps on replicating in your life, so that you are always prosperously happy.

"Great, great blessings and great, great happenings are always given to human mankind only through the magical word "Thank you".

Better absolute your feelings for this worldly life, so that you can ascend to great heights and experience the enchanting goodness meant only for you.

Learn the habit of "Thankfulness" to achieve all desired goals in your life. Choose not only happiness but also relate yourself to the self-endure nature of love, peace, success and achievement, which will carry your success to the divine heights.

Go to different places of happiness where it can transcend the nature of your life with a lot of goodness to capture all your best moments in life.

Set goals for your life with all good moments so that your gratitude nature continues to work for you in a better and better form. Work hard to keep your thankfulness to a greater extent of opportunity so that it takes you to the next level of highness in life. Feel the importance of **"Thank you"** to such a level that you do not have to do anything in life to reach the great height of success. You possess all the great power of love and compassion in the form of **"Thank You,"** which designates you to behave differently towards your life, where your achievement of your life cannot be stopped by anyone.

So please be in greater strength to capitalise all your wonderful, loving energy that you're surrounded by and living with. Particularly each and every moment of rejuvenation in your life is making everything much more possible to trust your activity.

Go to the great extent of knowledge, wisdom and skill, to possess yourself with thankfulness and greatness of all achievements. Do all that you can do without any hesitation and see how much you can proceed in the life you live, to bring back all the things you decide in your life. Achieve all the successful goals so that there are no limitations for any field of life. Provided you should be happy but put aside the knowledge of emotion that does not serve you anymore. Protesting your emotions will not do any great thing to your life, so carry on the way you feel that your life would be better for you.

Fall in love with the **"Thank you"** note that still loves you back without any regret. Carry on the way you are, so that it is not disturbing to you.

The premise of **"Thank you"** is not decided with any boundaries of achievement. It is yet a single word of trust and belief of goodness happening to you. You will always overflow with so much wonderfulness in your life that you will never realise what made all the good things come back to you. So do not regret anything in your life to capture what you left behind. You are always reminded that you are in the right place with the right opportunity and trust.

Get going on every step and edge of your life to achieve whatever you need to get. The word **"Thank you"** not only enchants you but also beautifies your life so wonderfully that you would never have to stop and look back at what you missed in life.

Achieve everything in life by just feeling and saying **"Thank you, Thank you"** at every great extent of your life. So do not bother for anything that will stop you from growing. You are already possessed by the word **"Thank you"** that will take you to every level of achievement.

Greater thankfulness is not only achieved but it can be attained with your life of love. Bring all the wonderfulness in life by the chant of "Thank you, Thank you, Thank you……."

Question yourself

1. What do you feel when you use the word thank you?
2. In which way gratitude has resolved your life problems?

Compassionate

Being compassionate is a method of knowledge, of showering love on others. It is the grace of love shown to others. Great love and awareness encompass the compassionate. It includes the richness of life with a love entity entrusted to others that you have. You will feel a great force of love and knowledge towards others. All the resources around you will tell the story of love and compassion.

Great things generally undergo a lot of pressure of love in order to prove their abundance. What else can be the idea of compassion to be showered on others? So, when there is a trigger of compassion in your body, you will feel and fall for it, not understanding why this is happening for you.

Let us understand the idea of compassion along with love, which can bring out the trust within each other. Some possible acts are about to happen within you, when you have realised that there is love for something known and unknown. Realisation of love and knowledge is very dull for everybody because of the sensitivity of the subject. Greater will be the love, the more you are compassionate towards others.

Are we living in love and compassion which is making life around us to survive with joyfulness and happiness?

The normality of compassion and the richness of compassion always flow through you in such a way that they are sometimes not realised within you. Why is it happening to me? The right knowledge of compassion is not understood by others since no one knows the real difference between love and compassion, so they can influence their life through it. In such cases, compassionate behaviour sometimes trends around to give the people knowledge of compassion.

Ok, as we keep on thinking of compassion, how do we show it to others with full trust? It must be made so simple that everyone carries the knowledge of compassion. Carry it in such a way that you will be thinking of it throughout the day.

It is fine to be told that love is not compassion. It is the love effect that rises within you unknowingly by looking at someone's situation. Suppose the person is surviving in a worse situation, it is then that compassion really happens to you. It is such a wonderful feeling to be understood, and fine to be unknown for others, so that it can be taken to another level of higher consciousness.

Greater feelings tend to be trusted within you, where you feel for yourself without understanding why it is happening to you. The best way to experience compassion of others or give others is meant to be giving and helping with love and grace. Kindness also can be understood by you. So at anytime, when you feel the real range of greater compassion towards anything, it will always take you to the next level.

Sometimes the level of compassion does not even rise even if the situation is going down. This happens usually due to the feeling you have in this situation; partial knowledge of compassion does not encourage you to love and feel that kindness you have for the people. So, carry on as you are now so that it will keep on growing inside like a small child.

Compassion needs to grow within every human in order to survive in this world peacefully and without disturbing anybody's life. You are about to influence something new to everyone which will startle their life in such a way that they realise that something good is about to happen for them. Rise for the love you have within yourself that shows its grace of understanding love. Also better have an idea what are the things to be entitled within compassion that you have within yourself.

Question yourself

1. What makes you feel more compassionate?
2. Being in compassion is a desire or decision?

Courage

The word **"Courage"** itself is so courageous when heard. The vibration that is enrolled within this word is so strong, where you can feel the powerful energy flowing through it. So, courage can be anywhere and in any form. You have to realise the range of your courage that flows inside your body, within every aspect of life.

Courageous acts are not carried out in every situation when not required, since it is not shown in every area of life. Courage is a natural being that is set within every person and is not known to all until and unless you realise the reality of life. A greater approach to courage is being entangled with the artificial feeling of strength along with fear. We need to know how much courage is needed in this particular situation. Everybody is not evolving through this courage, since many people lack a realisation of why this feeling is so courageous and significant.

It is to be understood that courage is inherently natural that is resting in your body without your knowledge. It will arise only through necessity, when really needed to win or overcome a situation.

You have always been chased through all situations of life which took you to every area of life it was only possible through your courage. There are many ways where our courage emerges when it is really needed for us to get over the situation successfully. There has also been a need to realise your courage in order to enhance your lifestyle.

It is very worthwhile for you to show courage really whenever you need it. Courage is the only survival part to entrust your life so that you can move forward to survive in this world.

"Courage not only gives you survival skills but it also builds the idea, how to handle the situation very skillfully and knowledgeable".

Normally, we all are courageous to have great strength to live this life in full of joy and happiness. But suddenly question arises, why is this happening to me? Is it necessary for me to have courage? Is it very necessary for me to live this life every minute courageously to survive human life? Yes, you need to be courageous in each and every part of life encompassing fear, fight, rage, unhappiness, wrong situations and everything that happens around you.

The great understanding of courage gives you more courage to surpass the feeling of strength that has been stored within you for so many days. Realising the extent of your strength is crucial, as it can help you in every situation. Just now is the right time for courage to rise from every part of the body since you have realised where the courage has been stored in your body. Greater idea of courage was not discussed earlier because it had no structure or a particular behaviour to perform in a particular way.

Ok, everything happens at your best moment that suddenly arises when a situation really needs courage. Gradual change in your attitude and bold behaviour is always welcomed in this courageous behaviour to transcend and show your behaviour of strength to everybody. So entrusting courage within yourself is nearly necessary for you at every stage of your life so that you can really live a very happy and good life.

Question yourself

1. What is your definition for courage?
2. Where is the courage in you?

Strength

"When the power of strength is rising up from your inner body, you have to realise that greater energy is going to show its abundance in the nature of its performance".

The real contrast in your life has always been your strength that has been hidden within you. You have to nurture your strength every time and whenever it is needed in your life. As you grow up in your life, you have to understand that the behaviour of your strength is always outpouring tremendously with the full power of knowledge of what you are doing in your life. When life takes you to a different situation and circumstance, you have to know that some power that is residing within you just brings a great bunch of knowledge to create a tremendous power of strength.

The power of strength is not only the mode of your life growth but it is also the great substance of existence in your real life itself. So generally, when you realise your real power of strength it has to be stimulated each and every time, whenever possible.

Casual life is always led with the strength of power to live each and every stage of your life. The great principle of strength cannot be hidden behind anything. It is such a good thing to achieve whatever you want in your life. Similarly, all the things that are happening around life boundaries are always induced or encouraged by the other external factors which keep on affecting your daily life.

The possibility of showing strength in a particular situation always wins small or large in the way you always want. Since you know that something that happened greatly has happened only through your strength. For the power of strength, you have to strengthen your physical and mental body to activate its greater power. This is to be done for the good reason of your life to prosper.

The strength of humans always differs from human to human. It is actually the inner feeling of showing how strong they are mentally and physically. In so many ways people show their strength in their own attitude which decides their level of performance. Since people's survival in this natural world is only through their real strength.

Strength is not only carried physically or mentally but it creates a great resistance for bringing any bad things to you, as you feel the strength energy rising to a greater extent. Your belief on living life also increases so tremendously that no one can stop you from moving to the next stage of your life.

"Strength is a sacred behaviour which leads to a lot of changes in your life without considering what is happening around your situation".

Fearless way to lead a life is only the inner strength that helps to remove everything from your life that is not necessary to be there for you.

Greatness of strength can be experienced only when you hit that target at the right point. It does not mean that your strength has to be flowing within you all the time. It can rise up when really necessary.

Feeling of strength has left many people so astounding in their life that it has brought greater changes in their life than expected. The tendency of strength is usually considered either physical or mental. But anyway, it can be possessed in your life when it is really needed.

Strengthening is more necessary for your will power than the physical body. As your will power gets strengthened, the thing that you want to achieve in your life becomes easier than the physical achievement. Here we can come to an understanding that in reality, every human living in this universe has to grow this power of strengthening day by day so that it can change the life of each person easily.

Goodness in every activity is also a strength that really needs to be played in life. Therefore, when the power of strength is rising up from your inner body you have to realise that greater power of energy is going to show the nature of its performance in abundance.

Greater the strength, greater is the achievement. In any case scenario, as you keep on strengthening and becoming more strengthened you will be able to do anything for your life without any struggle. In return, life always becomes as easy as you think. You will be receiving strength to play the life game very successfully in any situation.

It is a great advantage for you to be stronger in your strength, always ensuring an unstopping good and happy life. This is the only hope that nature keeps on giving to run your life so miraculously. Very easily and effortlessly, you can change yourself through the power of strength.

Question yourself

1. Do you need to strengthen your life every day and why?

2. Is strength for you physically or mentally?

Love

"The greatest attitude of love can be when you give it to others without expecting in return from others because it is not an investment to give you a return of interest. It is a saving which gives you a larger amount of richness in life, which makes you prosper throughout your lifetime".

Love is the emergency of opportunity to show others how much you like yourself and others. It does not display any attitude in your behaviour to showcase the love you have for others and yourself.

The term love cannot be defined appropriately as they are not definite to be explained for each and everyone. Since love varies from person to person, situation to situation and depending on other aspects of life. We all love ourselves in a certain way that is something running within us to promote likeness towards things we feel eternal.

Love cannot be distinguished or categorised between people, status, lifestyle, good and bad. It relays the same power from everyone when someone is in real love. The power of love does not estimate anything from anyone as there is no measurement scale of one's love.

In case you are willing to measure your love, there are no definite rules to explain, that this is the way to measure it.

Everyone finds love in some or the other case in every stage of their life.

Love is real life insurance when you are living with people you really love and care about. In every stage of life, love plays a very great role to display in one's life. How much love is important? Love is everything. There is no existence without love. No man or woman has escaped the frequency of love from their birth to death. Love effect is the greatest strength to change a person or a situation. Every human surely is in need of love to survive in this world. Love takes its own form to prosper in one's life.

No amount of love can provide a cheat code when the true power of love ignites. The experience of love is to be really experienced with intense energy of feeling within you. We don't know, why this love is so abundant and prosperous when felt, because it thrives solely only on the genuine feelings of people. As usual the feeling of love not only creates happy emotions or any other type of emotions but it makes you feel that everything is possible in life. Love makes your life easy and it reaps a good number of nice feelings within you.

As you grow older the love method or love emotion keeps on changing as per the feeling it has towards a concern or activity. Love is a major project activity when you want to love a person who is not really interested in you. It takes a lot of programming to love and show love to that person. The graciousness of love is so enormous when there is a great feeling that can be felt within you. There is also a need for love in everybody's life as it acts as a fuel to carry your life further.

Love is a true entity in this universe apart from anything you see, feel in this world. The strength of love is greater, because it can bring a magnificent change in any kind of person you want to love until and unless the person is not interested in you.

Feel the love where you are and what you are so that the survival of humans will become better and better.

Question yourself

1. Where is love hidden within you?
2. How supportive is your love to you?

Divinity

Divinity is above all the activities in this world. There is no discrimination between good and bad behaviour in order to fulfill divinity in your life. As you live the life of mankind you also need to try divinity so that it enhances your life structure and beautifies your life.

In case there is no divinity in your life there would not be any existence in this worldly life. Therefore, it is always necessary for you to follow a divinity lifestyle in order to support your living on this earth. Growth of life can only be possible when divinity arises in everything. There is also an allowance of divinity in this world so that you can thrive thoroughly.

Gradually people nowadays are changing themselves from divinity to technology to enhance their lifestyle, thinking that it would be the best way to survive in this world. These people will one day surely understand that this is not the correct path to lead life on earth.

Whenever there was a crisis in this world, people's escapism was only through the gateway of divinity. It was not a correct way to approach divinity but people did not know how to get out of their life problems. They imagine that their life can be saved only through divinity. Yes! It is true in the case of necessity but in reality, people do not really want to feel and follow divinity. Actually, it is the real way to get out of the problems and adverse circumstances.

There was always a certain amount of people who followed and taught divinity to the society so that the people can live their life peacefully. The divine people are those who really understand the real purpose of this life. These genuine people knew the real power of God / Universe, which had immense goodness of trust that enthroned great power of energy around the world.

The people have to understand that the great power on which the world lives and works is only through divinity, the energy that is vibrating throughout your lifetime. It is not said that divinity is God but it is like a power through which God was made so that people can understand - What is the energy that takes the form of God structure? The God structure not only enhances power but showcases the reality of life to run this world. There is more trust in God than divinity because people assume and think that God is divine but in reality, that is not the case.

Divinity is the greatest and highest power that is bestowed within you, that projects consciousness from you. The connection of the universe and you exists from birth to death in each body it has resided. God is the greatest form of divinity so that the people can realise that there is something higher than us which will take care and protect us to a greater extent in this life.

People really have not understood the great power of divinity since they did not realise and know what it really means. People always needed something to help them in a difficult situation or circumstance, when problems had to be solved. They believed this energy had great power to solve the problems whenever they prayed for it.

The real divinity is oneness of mind with the higher consciousness in the present moment and is called real divinity power. Divinity can help your life so easily when you come to an understanding that the nature of life cannot survive without divinity.

Every man and woman should be serving divinity in different forms from their own understanding. But they do not properly understand what they really need to know: What is the real divinity? What is the real great power hidden inside it? Each and every human being on this earth is needed to experience the godly divineness in their own way and understand what type of power is pouring in our life. The actual thought or feeling of divinity that humans can realise is only when they feel that energy of God or universe which is flowing within them is the real God.

All these years, humans had been searching for real God, to unite with oneness. He or she never really realises that God is always united with them and has always been the inner source. It is the real living God which can be felt and realised.

Every human has to somehow experience divinity in their lifetime without forgetting that every human itself is a divine energy that once actually came out of a larger divine energy source. So that they can serve their purpose on this earth, live with all good and bad things that they have done in their past life in the other universe or the same earth. Now after being born on the earth at least, they have to realise that divinity can be easily understood. They also believe that divinity is the real form of life, guiding them to go through life situations and helping them to transcend the unrealistic world which is surviving on these materialistic emotions.

Divinity is a must and the only thing that makes a human survive through all their life hardships and attains freedom from this life on earth.

Great changes are happening for a reason but humans have to understand that everything is happening only for their good. To sustain in this world happily, it is always good for everyone to follow and live with divinity.

Question Yourself

1. Did you feel divinity in your life?
2. What is divinity for you? Do you accept it?

Friendship

Great, great people had succeeded their life through friendship only, as they knew how to stay in a good friendship. We all might think that friendship is being friendly in the relationships you carry with others. It is not actually a relationship you have with others. It's a great relationship you have with yourself that is what is meant here as friendship. For having a friendship within yourself, you need not have an external person to soothe you or take care of you.

Friendship is how well you maintain a relationship with yourself and your soul. This friend cannot be seen but can be realised, felt within and get emotionally connected with you. Your friend knows who you are. It does not discriminate between ages, gender, status, life or anything in this world. It just looks at how well you stay connected with yourself by providing abundance of love and respect in the form of self-worth.

Your inner self always needs a lot of happiness, love and self-worthiness at every stage of your life. Do understand that no person is differentiated from their inner self but you are the oneness of yourself. There is no difference between you and yourself, but there is a lot of difference where humans show from their inner selves.

As you are not connected with the inner self, you slowly start to bring a lot of suffering and pain into your life. It is really important that each and every person on this earth needs to realise that every person on earth has to get connected with their inner self, which cannot be seen but can be felt and realised when you get connected with it in oneness.

You always look for great friendship in your life from humans. Many people do not get genuine friendship and always get cheated in many ways, losing the hope of people around them. Friendship within you is also a great relationship, like any other relationship. When you realise that, you will be ready to face any sort of future life.

You just need to realise that your inner self is always waiting to get connected to you and want to speak with you at each and every moment of life, but the humans do not realise that someone within ourselves is trying to always get connected with us.

You need no external person to guide you, to protect you, and to encourage you. This one inner self is more than enough to play a different role to keep you safe, protected and guided at each and every moment of your life. Whatsoever circumstances you are going through, just stay always connected with your inner self that is more than enough to change your life.

There have been a lot of great changes in people who had great friendships with their inner self. These people have always been a great success in their life with a lot of happy moments. They would have already realised that there is nothing more important in this world than being connected with one self. This friendship of the inner self connection is more than enough for each and every human being, to stay focused and to live a happy life here after.

Human has to come to a great realisation that this life cannot be changed until and unless an individual realises that the greatest friendship is nothing, but the conscious connection within you is the ideal part of human life to be followed and cherished.

Let every human get a chance to realise that one protector, one guide, one advisor who exists within everyone is our real friend, who stays within you from the time you were born until your death.

As we say, that inner consciousness is the real consciousness of every human being since it has been so necessary to surpass each and every moment of human life very peacefully. It is really necessary for each and every one to get connected as soon as possible and start growing your friendship with oneself in order to live a happy life on this earth.

Question yourself

1. Which is your real friendship that makes you understand life?

2. How deep is your friendship within you?

Self-Discipline

The attitude of self-discipline cannot be measured or taught by anyone. It is only a method where one can follow by themselves to a very great extent. When there is self-discipline in one's own life, everything changes to a very great height, not only so they keep shifting their identity of living from one level to another.

There has been a great advantage to showcase one's self-discipline through only the life they are living. It is not money or status or education they have earned throughout the lifetime but a concept for own life where they can have a peaceful and loving life.

As far as possible one's life possibility with good behaviour and attitude of living a better life always comes from their own discipline. Greater the self-discipline greater is the life. He or she does not need to prove one's life on this earth. Humans born on this earth can come forward with different forms of habits and behaviour but one who corrects themselves in every step of life will become a successful living person.

Self-discipline of oneself has to come from within a person who is interested to change their life at any cost. Nobody can force a person to be self-disciplined since one has to think and understand that self-discipline is very much needed to survive in this life.

"A major definition of self-discipline can also be said that - Humans desire under a controlled thought and action towards their life without hurting others".

Every person who wants to build a self-disciplined life needs to start from the basic level of their life. Every small stage and step you take should be in a righteous way which gives a result of satisfaction to your own life.

So as to start with self-discipline, mankind has to see in what ways one can keep them self in a good and happy condition by building their discipline habits. You need to take a lot of actions in order to grow and build your discipline, behaviour and everything from small to big or up to down. Everyone should analyse that following all these step-by-step attitude would give them a better future.

Lot of understanding is needed while self-disciplining oneself. They need not copy the disciplining habit of another but they can understand and realise what type of activity will keep them fine. Self-discipline shapes a person's nature to a very great extent of what you did not expect. It shapes your behaviour, attitude, status, love, compassion, and everything from your personal to external life.

It is a great life changing victory for one's life when you are self-disciplined. So now onwards build certain habits of life to nurture your behaviour with self-discipline habits and methods that in return will always take care of you in a better way.

To understand,

Self-discipline = Success in personal life

Each and every person in this world has to understand, that the ignition of self-discipline in a person has to starve very hard in building their specialised habits. Finally, these habits will take care of you. The habits are your self-discipline activity that will later make you what you are.

Question yourself

1. Why is it necessary to be disciplined?
2. Has anything in your life changed due to self-discipline?

Happiness

Happiness is one of the greatest and the best attributes in every person's life. Each and every human living in this world should give greater importance to one's own happiness than making others happy. No human has survived in this world without feeling happiness in their life. The greatest achievement should be happiness that has changed one's life completely. No one in this world can live this life without happiness.

People always assume that happiness is like a drug to keep them moving to the next stages of life but yet no person shows the significance of being happy in a day-to-day life. Every person has to realise that they have to get trained themselves to be happy. Men and women of the world always keep searching happiness externally and finally fail to reach the destination of happiness. As per the human soul its greatest requirement is happiness. It always wants to be happy, all the time.

But many do not realise the power of happiness believing that it will not change their life. There has been a lot of philosophy, stories and other things describing ways to be happy. But yet no one tries to identify and becomes happy. Because it has become so complicated for each and every human being to think that being happy at all times is a really difficult task.

Human has not realised that happiness resides within oneself. It is not to be searched anywhere, rather be satisfied and have a gratitude mindset to always be happy. Practicing happiness has to be done by everyone to keep life going. Happiness is a marvellous feeling that affects you to a very great extent.

Happiness is the key to success. Nobody ever realises that life becomes so easy when happiness enters your life. Everything in life gets manifested easily. So, practice happiness by using different assistance to always keep you happy internally, not externally.

There has to be a very good practice to regularise the habit of developing happiness all the time. Bring all the good opportunities through the emotion of happiness. Just laughing and smiling does not bring changes in your life. But true happiness is when your inner self starts recognising and feeling it, where it stays in blissful moments all the time and every time.

At no cost, you can set up happiness by a lot of gratitude. Being thankful is one of the best things for the source to feel happy. Let the soul of human possess greatest happiness in order to prosper in an easy and effortless life.

Question yourself

1. Is happiness a culture or habit for you?
2. What are your best experiences of happiness?

Positive Thinking

It is such a good thing to always be in a positive mindset. Bringing a positive mindset is possible only through positive thinking.

Each and every moment you need to keep on thinking positive even if the situation does not support you. You need to find positivity in every aspect of life but it is quite difficult for everyone since many people do not know how to feel or think positive even in the worst-case scenario.

Most feel positivity only by speaking positively but they undergo a lot of pressure and stress to keep themselves in a positive mindset and also want to show others that he or she is always living a good, positive life. A positive thinking is not to show others your validation. But it is your present feeling of being right in any situation, as you embrace the thought of being positive and staying positive.

Explore your mind with different aspects of how to keep yourself in positive thinking which beholds good thoughts. Greater positive thinking, greater is the life. Train yourself every day, from one small moment to moments of positive thinking, so that this habit will become a great habit for you to flourish with positive thinking forever.

Thinking positive doesn't mean that negativity or the wrong side of life doesn't exist. It always happens that life is full of ups and downs, but whenever an adverse situation comes up, every human being needs to believe that something positive always exists in every situation. Therefore, it is necessary for each person to reintroduce positive thoughts into in their life. It can be done only by being conscious of the thoughts you are receiving.

Carry the habit of being conscious to yourself to build a positive attitude, little by little without pressuring yourself. Let everything happen with a flow so that you will find it easy to develop positive thinking.

Thinking positive is a great pleasure for one who has practiced it very thoroughly because he or she knows how beautiful their life would be and how easier life may become.

Great people, renowned people and many successful people attribute their achievements, only to positive thinking, that led them to a life of achievement and success. Infact earlier also, great people would have found it difficult to build a habit of positive thinking, but the urge to win their life must have led them to positive thinking.

Even though, so many people have succeeded through positive thinking, many don't think or live believing that thinking positively will yield them success. Most don't even realise that the main root of success is their own positive thought that has boomed their life, to greater heights of success and good fortune.

So hence, whatever be the life you live or travel, it is necessary for each and every person to enhance positive thinking. Positive thinking must become compulsory in order to live a beautiful and happy life.

Question yourself

1. Why is it important to build positive thinking?
2. What changes were influenced by positive thinking in your life?

Evaluate

Evaluate each understanding of your life. Never underestimate any situation, circumstance for any reason. Every incident is trying to communicate something or the other, so it is always necessary for us to evaluate every step of life.

Being casual or forgetful does not give you any possibility of goodness. It is to be considered under the possibility of living under the circumstances of fate. Let us realise that there is no situation that has not been realised at any time. Everyone tries to improve the situation for better with or without knowing because everyone is striving to live a good life.

Evaluation of situation becomes necessary for each and everyone's life, when human beings are looking for betterment in their life. Evaluation of situation does not give any formula to live but it comes to an understanding, that there is a chance in every way to live life happily. As you understand the importance of living life happily, you will try to evaluate your life, love and considerations.

Evaluation is really needed for betterment in life even if your outer circumstances are not proper. Do understand that inner evaluation is very necessary, nothing starts from outside. Evaluate, how you feel inside, each and every moment you are living on this earth.

Don't try to leave the inner feelings in ignorance. If you are ignorant, it means you are very careless thus hindering the pursuit of living a good life.

It is really very necessary for every inner feeling to be analysed and evaluated with deeper understanding and connections. As you start to evaluate each and every situation from your inner self, you will very soon realise that the external world of your life, only exists within your inner self.

So you need to understand that when your inner self is happy and feeling good, your outside or the external world changes immediately and you don't even realise what is happening so quickly. Everything will change with reference to your thoughts and feelings.

Keep the evaluation of life like a habit, so that one day it will become your character through-out your lifetime and you do not need to run back from anything, in search of happiness and prosperity in life.

So being grateful for each and every activity you do in your life, as well as, whatever you keep receiving is always the best return of evaluation. To keep your family life as well as your inner self happy, feel and start to show gratitude, for the life you have been given and for the inner self living within you.

Do not engage in a lot of unnecessary entertainment in order to keep yourself stress free. Summing up, if you try and evaluate, you will realise how much you have bothered your life with careless decisions.

Question yourself

1. Do you evaluate every step in life?
2. In what way would you evaluate your life?

Respect

"Respect for oneself is the real jewel of your life you need to wear, carry and live with."

"RESPECT", the word is so challenging when you hear it. It's a showcase work on one self and others.

It is said that respect is a great feeling for somebody you have within yourself, with no idea of what he or she is doing. The word respect does not need any dignity to be shown, even if there is a requirement. It is already a very sensitive word which has been formulated in every situation as per requirement. There is no need for any measurement you need to have to respect a person. It is a sensual way to show your grace with a good feeling and let that person know what type of attitude you carry towards them.

Respect can gain a lot of weight as your respect flows towards a concern. There are some differences in respect when you show it forcefully on others and when you show respect on others with love.

When you really have respect for the person, you really like, it can really make you feel happy from your inner emotion. Sometimes you don't realise, why you respect a person without any reason, it happens suddenly when you have respect for a person due to some forcible thoughts or ideas that have earlier been sown in your mind.

Respect is not necessarily needed for the other person. It can also be given to oneself for what you are. It really should be a compulsory habit of respecting yourself. None other than you need to be respected by yourself because in this world, you are the real person who needs to be respected all the time. It must be the most desired habit of every human being, to respect oneself with great self-esteem and love.

So, it is necessary for every individual to follow a respectful behaviour in every stage of life. Even if you are not in a good condition, respect is the only attitude which portrays of how a human being is from inside and out. It does not depend on his or her work, status, richness and the type of wealth you have. Summing up the respectful behaviour, you have to come to an understanding of the real value of what you carry to watch yourself throughout your lifetime.

Better to be in a conscious mode, so that you are able to activate your behaviour each and every time and all the stages of life. You should not forget how valuable a person you are on this earth.

Question yourself

1. How much do you respect yourself?
2. Do you measure the respect others give you?

Delightful

Being delightful means to feel and be in pleasure, when you are immensely involved in an activity. It is such a great feeling of wonderfulness, without realising what is happening to us externally. Delightfulness is a type of happiness that makes you feel very good wherever you go. Delightfulness does not happen regularly, but it is to be feeling happy on a regular basis.

The gracious feeling of oneness with any situation, a person, or an incident feels like you are fulfilled from every side. Right from the bottom of your heart, that's a deep feeling of pleasure, that sprouts out on a very great height and the person around you also feels the same feeling you have.

The state of being pleasurable in a situation without discrimination of good or bad and which creates happiness without understanding can be termed as delightfulness. Every human has to go through these types of delightful situations in their life, even without realizing why they are feeling happy. There are a lot of great changes, as the person enjoys the delightful situations in their own way.

An expected pleasure makes you very happy, as that of an unexpected situation because every human is trying to find a situation to keep themselves happy. It is like a stage of ecstasy and happiness mixed cultural behaviour, where even sometimes you don't know what is happening around you.

The greater you feel delighted, the more pleasure and happiness rush from the depth of your heart. It is really a great attitude for being delighted since it increases every situation into happiness, without finding any fault with the situation. Being in high stages of delightfulness, a human never stays in their own thoughts, but stays conscious and understands that pleasure has occupied their mind, and they will more consciously enjoy that situation without any second thought.

There has always been a great hope of happiness that humans have always wanted to experience. One of the major things is that a human can feel delighted without expecting anything from others.

Delighted people are the ones who are extremely in love with the situation and want that situation to happen more and more. So, there is great need for delightful situations for everybody in this world.

Question yourself

1. What does it mean to you to be delighted?
2. Have you created any delightful situations again and again?

Appreciate

"Appreciating and being appreciated is such a beautiful way of giving and receiving compliments of love and gratitude, and at the same time, it will bring a great change in life".

Appreciation is a gracious way of praising someone, about whom you feel very good. It feels so nice when we are being praised even though there is no evidence of performance from our side.

Receiving praise just like that or for hard work, both give immense pleasure to the person who hears and receives it. You feel you are at the top of the world; you feel that nothing can stop you from reaching your goal. It is really a good phase when a person is really appreciated, as it takes them to a greater level of achievement. The attitude while appreciating others is a good and a praiseworthy thing because you need to put out or be away from your ego to feel happy and appreciate others.

Appreciation always gives great hope to all the people who all are listening. It does not discriminate between known and unknown people; it is only a way to show gratitude to another person for their performance, which might be great or not. So, when we deliberately appreciate a person, it actually changes the present situation into a graceful circumstance, feeling that everything around you is also happy.

It has always been nice to understand that appreciating others is such a beautiful act to undergo in order to change and bring happiness to a person. Appreciation actually motivates a person, if they are really appreciated from the bottom of the heart. While receiving appreciation, it gives a feeling of fulfillment in the act of doing something, and also feels that the individual action, has added some benefit to other beings. It is natural that appreciation can make and bring miracles into a person's life, even if they have not performed very big.

The act of appreciation should also be appreciated because without any prior acquaintance he or she is willing to appreciate a person, feeling that they have done something good. It feels nice when you try to appreciate a person. It not only makes you happy for appreciating others, but even the receiving person will reflect the same happiness, that you have. Feeling of happiness from deep inside your heart is a great sense of bliss, which happens when appreciation is received and given.

"There cannot be less or more appreciation to make a person happy. It is only the receiving end of how they respond to appreciation".

The greatness of appreciation should always be cherished and felt even if you have not done any appreciation towards anybody. You need not have great courage or words to appreciate a person. It can be a simple gesture or behaviour where it shows, that the person near to you has done a great job, which will be very good for a happy moment.

If you need your life to be very easy and to go on with a lot of goodness, it is simple to appreciate others without putting your ego first. Keep aside the entire attitude that does not give you space to appreciate others. As you appreciate you will start having great changes too and also will be receiving immense gratitude from other people.

So be nice to others. Receiving a lot of appreciation for goodness will always motivate you to move to the next step of living a beautiful and wonderful life. Always be ready to appreciate others, whenever you have the chance to do it.

Attitude of appreciation with love, kindness, happiness and goodness towards your own family makes you more prosperous in your life.

Question yourself

1. What do you appreciate about yourself?
2. What is your level of appreciation for others?

Relationship

Relationship is a kind of attachment that is held between one or many people, something that happens willingly or unwillingly.

Having a very good relationship with a person is a great chance for a human to be happy on earth. All relationships have one or the other purpose to serve each other. Every relationship needs to understand, that there should not be any compulsion between the persons, who have a close relationship in order to sustain it. A relationship should not exist for the sake of love, status, money or other external sources which are required to keep two or more persons happy. It should not be a compulsion to live life with another person in order to maintain a relationship, even though it does not provide happiness.

Most of the people have respect only towards the status of their life, they are living. It should not possess any type of pressure between people to exist in a good relationship. All kinds of relationships have some kind of bonding with or without any respect.

Many people are compelled to carry the relationship, with the person who is not good for their life. There is always a great responsibility when you are in a relationship, especially regarding gender respect. The attachment in a relationship exists in a very great range for a real relationship or a relationship carried with compulsion.

There are a variety of relationships that have been built over years in the name of status, religion, money and sacrifice, which does not make any human relationship happy at all, but there is a great deal of understanding between two or more people. Suppose a relationship exists but there is no understanding, what is the need to live like this. It has no meaning to a relationship, knowing that they have wasted so many years.

Relationships nowadays have become a gross benefit in the name of money, status and society. Nobody understands the real consciousness that exists between relationships. Every relationship always outlines a community of oneness but for some, there doesn't exist a great value and respect.

Before being into a relationship of love, family and other types, one has to understand that, every relationship always starts with some expectation, which can be fulfilled by the other person. Being closer in a family, friends or any other bond, does not define a relationship to be perfect. But always carries the feeling, that there exists someone in their life. Before being or exiting from any relationship you should always come to an understanding that life is always bound in relationship in the universe. And every relationship always exists to help each other to live a better life in a happy manner.

It is better to celebrate any kind of relationship you have around, since it has a very great value until you exist on this earth, which you do not realise until you lose it.

Question yourself

1. What is the relationship between you and yourself?
2. The best way you achieved your important relationship (yourself/others)?

Forgiveness

"Forgiveness is the key to the greatest treasure box of happiness. It is the main key which opens the door to happiness without any regret".

"Forgiveness" is the greatest attitude of human life. There cannot be an alternative for forgiveness, to make something better in your life. As you learn to forgive things, life around you always change.

Many do not realise the power of forgiving people because of their ego. They do not want to step down from the ego and forgive others, since they think that it loses one's own self-esteem.

Great, great people learned the trick to keep themselves very happy and peacefully, by forgiving and forgetting what others had done to them. Once forgiveness is practiced in life, you never need to go in search of a solution for a problem. It is the easiest way to rectify your life from guilt, fear, stress and depression.

Forgiveness gives you the freedom of being captive in the thoughts of others. You need not bestow forgiveness in the usual process. You can just do it in your mind by just imagining that you are forgiving that person and letting go the situation. This type of a process of forgiving, will be an immense turning point in your life.

It will cure all diseases, guilt, and stress, and if there are some other types of issues, you will be rid of them.

The great moment of forgiveness, is the feeling of inner peace within you, when you will forgive others. And apart from it you need to forgive yourself, for what all happened in your past. You play an important role in case of any issues that are happening in your life.

So be very stringent in forgiving yourself and others. It plays a great role in transforming your life and taking your life to the next level. It is better to catch the feeling of peace within yourself, by forgiving others and yourself.

Learn as well as, teach the forgiveness attitude around you, so that as you teach the path of happiness, you will always be happy. Practice every day without forgetting, that you will always and daily bring a magnificent change in your life through forgiveness.

Once the habit of forgiveness gets attached to your brain you will soon realise the power, that is evolving inside the word "FORGIVENESS" and that power can be only realised when you really forgive people deeply from your heart. You will really feel that your heart has become empty and clear. All your worries, stress, everything will be just blown away just like that and will bring the feeling of inner peace within yourself.

Don't just take anything for granted. The behaviour of forgiveness is so magnificent, that it can change one's life tremendously. Learn to catch the best part of your forgiveness, so that you will learn to understand, how it not only changes your life but also the person you forgave will also start to shower love on you.

The result of forgiveness should be experienced by every individual in this world, in order to feel the great system of happiness. The best part of forgiveness is that it is the easiest way to find peace within yourself, when you are ready to forgive, without any attitude of human behaviour.

Question yourself

1. Is forgiveness a boon or punishment for you?
2. Mention a person or situation which you want to forgive in life?

Attitude

"As humans move away from the reality of their life, they also move away from the awareness of life in order to play a false role in this universe".

Great personalities have shown an act of their behaviour in the form of attitude. It is also sometimes taken into consideration that people being famous or well-known possess some type of behaviour impact called attitude.

Each and every human on this earth possesses some or the other type of attitude, which makes them different and can be distinguished between each and every people. Great, great legends with different attitudes are said to have a habit of behaviour, which has made them reach a great height in their life. As per concerned with the type of people's behaviour and attitude, there is always a great difference in range from situation to situation and from person to person. It is also sometimes considered as arrogance with their kind of behaviour but in fact it is the real attitude of behaviour of that concerned person.

Attitude is actually a kind of behaviour or approach of a person where they feel comfort in showing their intentions to others. So there never lies any mistake in the attitude of a person since that person feels good with their behaviour. Carrying a good, impressive attitude always does good things to the concerned person. Since people around will feel good, to stay along with the person with the right attitude.

Situations or circumstances always keep changing a person's attitude. Most of the common people are forced to have a good, decent attitude to impress people around them. When the real attitude is suppressed, the human tries to put a false act on themselves. Not only does an individual change their real attitude, but in fact, the person becomes compelled to change one's reality.

The ordinary person perceives that the people with great attitudes are meant to be rich and arrogant. People with different higher status display their attitude proudly and openly to show their reality of how they are along with that and they think that there is no necessity to show false behaviour or attitude.

As you keep on building an attitude with a good sense of awareness and consciousness, you will also start feeling that you are living the life you want, very happily and graciously.

Attitude or behaviour, whatever a human may perceive, they should be in strong realisation of understanding that no attitude shows them the actual reality until and unless there is existing awareness. It is better to have a comfortable lifestyle in order to live your life with ease. Building an attitude from a young age knowingly and unknowingly makes some people's life difficult. Let's teach the people around us what type of attitude makes them live the life they want in that happy moment. Simplifying the attitude behaviour always gives you a happy real life without bothering and disturbing people around you.

Carry the type of attitude where people feel good to stay and enjoy your presence. So, a better and neat behavioural attitude always lets you live the life you wish and always makes you feel better at every stage.

Choose your attitude to reach great heights in your life so that, there might be great opportunities flowing into your life incessantly.

Question yourself

1. How does your attitude influence your life?

2. What are you and your attitude?

Simplicity

"The greatest opportunity for mankind to show their realistic being can be only through simple behaviour, attitude and thought".

Simplicity is the one of the greatest pieces of evidence of life, how a person lives.

It is always said that great people are always simple, which means they won the path of life through the simplicity of living. Even if a person earns a large amount of money or lives in a great fame, only the person with their real simplicity always wins life.

There have always been a lot of turning points, when you decide to follow a simple life. There might be a great resistance or hindrance to your growth, but once you have realised that a person with simplicity always understands life, you also decide to live in a realistic, normal way. As you try to turn yourself into a simple being, it is understood, that you are bound to have a lot of good things to receive.

However, our society and this world believe only in flaunting a high status, people those who show off are real celebrities in this world. But actually, simplicity is to have a better living and good future throughout their lifetime.

It is better to understand, that being simple always makes one person's life more and more humble and easy to live. The humans under the balance of simplicity really stay in awareness, to lead a life very peacefully. As you understand the power of simplicity, you know that being conscious of following simplicity will bring a lot of wonderfulness in your life.

As you know, less wants or very few desires always gives you little expectation and more peace. The person who follows simplicity always lives a peaceful and happy life unconditionally because they have nothing to lose.

There are many ways, where you can follow simplicity. One might dress in a very simple manner, one does not want to show off, display status, etc. Different people have their own ways of following simplicity, where they do understand that being simple makes their life easier and better in this world.

Simplicity has always given more goodness to an individual where one lives. Every human has to realise that, in the universe nothing is real except the soul and that is life inside you. When you come to this awareness of life, you will considerably change your way of life and will surely live a better, happy and a peaceful life.

Question yourself

1. Do we actually need simplicity?
2. Your view on simplicity?

Focus

"As you blend yourself with the situation of your intention, you will always draw yourself too close to what you want to achieve".

Focus on what type of life you are living and will be living for the future. Focus has a very great importance towards attainment of one's goal. Full focus on the desire you want to manifest, will arrive soon, when the focus is consistent. Greater the focus, greater is the achievement.

Full knowledge of focus, is little known by human beings. Actually, humans do not realise the power of focus because they are not aware of it. As your focus goes off as your mind wanders, it will not be kept in one place since it does not know how it works behind your life and what type of energy, you release. But unaware of that, people focus on a lot of negative things that are happening around them.

Even though they sometimes realise that always thinking about negative thoughts does not yield good results, they are still captured in mind control. As you are caught, within your mind you will not be able to see any situation that is taking your life in the wrong direction. Gradually when you focus on unwanted things, they easily get manifested and unhappy situations come into your life. Repeated exercise of the same or focusing on unwanted thoughts, always generate issues that make your life more critical.

Most successful people in the world are very focused on what they want in their life. They have strong desires with focused intentions. Their focused intentions always lead them to get different opportunities, in order to successfully fulfill their goals.

As you exercise and practice focus day by day, you will start observing changes in yourself and you will understand how your life has transformed. Anyone who focuses on what work they are doing and feeling, they will keep moving to the next level of their life.

Life's circumstances always keep on giving greater knowledge to focus and navigate the life you wish. It becomes very easy for a person to reach and attain their goal as expected.

Being focused is nothing but being conscious through awareness. It is a great practice to give one's full attention to a desire, which will have greater achievement in their life.

Focusing is a very crucial topic because nothing in this world is achieved without focus. A lot of focusing habits need to be practiced by each and every human being in their life otherwise their life will not give the results they are looking for. Make a little habit of focusing each day it will give a great life in your upcoming future. Gradually life comes to an understanding that a person with greater focus always gets into a good condition in life, and is able to draw all the needs, wants and opportunities they wish to achieve.

Focus on one great thing, which will always intend you to do great things in your life. The practice is must for each and every being and it is very important to understand how life around them revolves and evolves.

Question yourself

1. How do you focus on life?
2. What are the ways to learn to focus?

Character

Character is a design of a human behaviour, how a human act and behaves in all the situations of their life. A character can be inborn or can be self-made on the basis of their lifestyle.

As you grow old, some of the characters keep changing due to the situation you have been influenced by. Most people have a belief system that the character of a person is designated through their life's status, that they have procured from childhood. It is sometimes true that certain people own the character, from the birth itself.

Characteristic behaviour always refers to an individuality of what type of a person, he or she would be. Many habits are practiced by people as they travel in life.

A character of a person has a great impact on the society and the family they are living in, because people believe certain things are appreciated and certain are not. So having good manners is generally taken for greater consideration. A person with good discipline and higher behaviour is believed to be successful.

Character of a person has nothing to do with success and failure because character does not design one's own life. But a character with proper discipline, always receives good respect from the people around you. The characters when displayed in this world, in different forms, always have a contradictory feeling.

People with good character are said to have disciplined habits, which always result in the betterment of their own life. A good character can always be formed through disciplinary habits that are followed by the person on a regular basis. Many habits of good discipline and behaviour are necessary to show greater results of your character.

Actually, character building is a long route, which requires dedication and effort rather than seeking the easiest path. As your thoughts appear, it always puts that into action and that gradually turns into habit, when it is often repeated again and again. It gets registered as a habit into one's subconscious mind. With or without knowing people draw their character from the habits, that they have been repeating for a long period of time. So, always be careful with the thoughts you possess and beliefs because each single thought, builds a characteristic in your life, that too very easily, without your knowledge.

It is a great advice for everyone, to always have a conscious thought in life at every stage in order to have a good character.

Character of any high status person, is always given very due respect because people believe that a person with good and disciplined character has led life to happiness and peace along with success, as long as they lived. Characters can be generalised but every character should be developed in a very special manner, so that they are able to live an extraordinary life.

Question yourself

1. Is your character creating your own life?
2. Which is the most inspiring character that has influenced your life?

Purpose

"Purpose" the word itself questions yourself being self-realised for what you have to do at that moment. Everything has a reason or purpose, for us to perform a particular act in a situation. It is the act of performing a particular activity, for a period of time until you're on this earth.

Every person deserves and possesses the purpose to live in this world. But very few come to realise - What type of activity are they doing on this earth? Why have they come to the earth to perform a particular action? The whole set of humans on this earth have something to perform in order to help other people live a very beautiful life.

Everyone has come to this world to help each other, to live their life in this world happily. It is very necessary for every human to come to an understanding and should have compulsion to understand: Why we are born here and what is the purpose behind our survival on this earth?

It is always meant and understood that everything happens for a purpose on the earth. That means each and every action you perform or see holds a particular meaning that does not come to our understanding - Why has it really happened?

There always arises a big question:

Why is it happening in this way?

Who is making it happen?

We really need to realise that something is making everything correctly on purpose.

Our human life is given a purpose to perform on this earth, which helps other people live happily. Many people do not even know that there exists a purpose. They believe that they have to make money and live life only through enforcement of other people's wish. Some people do not even realise that they are living their life for other people's happiness. In this case there is no awareness and no realisation that they are working for the happiness and benefit of others.

Every mankind has to search and realise the purpose as soon as possible, in order to serve the humanity on the earth which will always benefit the person with good fortune.

Living with purpose or living a purposeful life is really a blessing for the people, who have really realised that because it will give them peace of mind, joy and happiness throughout their lifetime till they live on this earth. As you serve people with a purpose of helping, it will always give you a better and a rich life and also it will bring prosperity at each step and every moment of your life. It would be better if these humans are forced to realise their purpose of life and the job that is assigned for them in this lifetime.

Knowing your purpose of life is really important in a very great manner. It always lets humans live a life of real achievement with greater understanding and joy. Understand your purpose and pursue it at the earliest in order to become a good human.

Question yourself

1. Did you try to know your purpose?
2. Are you ready to pursue your purpose?

Sympathy

Having sympathy for others is a godly trait. It does not differentiate any person on this emotion.

Everyone has a different way of showing sympathy to the people they care about. Sometimes sympathy rises unknowingly, without any evidence of attachment, just by hearing, seeing something which is unkind or feeling sorry for the situation. This world is working on sympathy and love for people that we have for each other. Sympathy is still very largely working on each and every person and it triggers their emotions. As in case of sympathy the person feels deeply hurt in concern to the subject, who is suffering and trying to help the other person to come out of the adverse situation.

Apart from sympathy nothing survives in this world because everyone is helping the other one only because of sympathy that you have. Sympathy exists in every place and situation to make mankind survive on this planet.

Unexpected events of sympathy have led humans to be tough at certain places, where emotions have left no love or care for anyone. But under the human heart there is always a feeling of sympathy to help and care for others. It is always said that we should be caring for others, since mankind is born to help each other without looking for any favour in return. Many people from generation to generation are only surviving through the sympathy of others for their livelihood.

Sympathy need not be taught to any one because it is an emotion that is embedded within everyone. It can only be triggered in the situation of hurt and pain. But certain people are sympathetic, they are mindful of how they can help and make others life better. There are many people in the world, who are still working to make the world a better place for humans to live happily.

Let sympathy rise in every situation, for every person so that we can bring an end, to any suffering and make this planet a place of happiness. Don't let sympathy diminish by keeping emotions locked and not realising when to show sympathy and provide help to mankind.

In many areas of life we need to trigger and teach people that a lot of sympathy is needed to make humans live happily. Don't lock all emotions inside you so that at the time of need the same sympathy will help you to come back again and change everything, letting you live a new life.

Have sympathy to live, grow and to be happy with all mankind.

Question yourself

1. Why is sympathy important to you?
2. Does sympathy change your behaviour?

Pleasure

Pleasure is a different type of happiness that makes even a single part of the cell vibrate at a particular frequency. To be very accurate, it is an individual's blissful happiness which takes them to a great height of feeling happiness and along with that the body vibrating in different frequencies.

For each individual pleasure always differs in a very different way. When a person feels pleasure within themselves on certain activities, it breaks them to cry out of all their feelings from the inside.

Being in all time, in pleasure is quite inevitable for everyone. It is a source of energy that brings the highest mood of enjoyment without disturbing anyone.

The great sense of pleasure in raising oneself with different actions can be appreciated because every human has accumulated so much pain or sadness in one's own life, which never lets them to enjoy any kind of happiness in their life. Every part of human life has a different attitude to perform their emotions in their own kind.

In their own way, the mankind tries to keep themselves happy in certain ways of pleasure by engaging in different activities. Everything can be pleasurable depending upon the mind of a person. Small kids find pleasure in toys, adults find pleasure in relationships or certain other things that make them feel more liberated and happier.

Humans search for happiness as a mood of pleasure through external factors. They never realise that pleasure has to be found inside themselves without looking for any external factors. All sources that are available nowadays for humans are good enough to give them pleasure personally. Every community finds the ways to bring pleasure in life with activities for every age group. Certain habits and activities are performed in order to let humans find their happiness in different forms.

Greater the pleasure, greater the richness they experience in life through their emotions. Every human has a certain amount of freedom to enjoy the richness of pleasure in hope of living life with greater goodness. It is also very much appreciable to humans on this earth. Most people do not even know that there exists a word called pleasure.

The most unique aspect of pleasure is the attitude of a person, with the combination of emotion in the correct level of output always generating good, memorable, pleasurable moments for a person.

Pleasure is a pure emotion, that touches you so deeply when you cannot stop having it again and again. So having a pleasurable life is very normal for humans. There is nothing so disgraceful in mentioning **"PLEASURE"**.

Let there be the existence of pleasure in every person's life with some disciplined habit that will always give you a good sense of pleasure. Feel greater to be a human with good beneficial discipline pleasure.

Question yourself

1. Is it possible to be in pleasure always?
2. How do you feel at that moment when you are in pleasure?

Beautify

"Live life in your own beautification on purpose so that you will have satisfaction in every stage of life".

Beautification of one's own life is a skilled art for an individual who realises and desires to live a life the way they want to live. There could be a lot of differences in many people's lifestyle, the way they want to live but whoever has decided to live their life in a particular way has greatly changed their future.

Defining beautification on one's self development is the aspect on which they decide to live their entire life for their own happiness. Beautify is a personal step one has to take at each and every moment of their life. It is very simple to live how you want to live, without fulfilling others' expectations.

No one can satisfy a human expectation to embody others happiness because all human's expectations keep changing from time to time, based upon their own requirements. When you personally want to beautify your own life, become a little selfish in a way where you paradoxically turn selfless to keep yourself very happy. Greater the knowledge of self-happiness, more the humans will beautify their life without any compromise. As you can afford your own happiness without any expectation of materialistic happiness, it always generates a greater beautification in every stage of life.

One's own life is a greater opportunity, to live with full understanding where they can beautify their life with love, happiness, peace, good relationship, health and prosperity. Beautification does not need a particular definition, it is only art of carving one's own life with the best self-development attitude and behaviour which reflect all the best things in their life, that mankind has been looking forward to.

Greater views with a lot of higher consciousness thoughts, combined with positive feelings will generate a beautiful life for you. Everyone has the right to own such a good life to live in this universe. No one needs to be limited by defining how to live their own life.

Every individual who has decided to live the life on their own discipline method, by unlocking all their own happiness, is how they want to spend their future. It is such a wonderful generosity, in living their own life, how they need to live will be a greater achievement for every individual.

No one knows or dictates a human's life beautification because each individual on this earth has a certain way of expectation to live their life to the best of knowledge. Everyone should plan daily and live to beautify their happiness and joy that can be found in every stage of their life.

As usual, there can be ups and downs in human life where one's own karma plays a great role. Also, you learn to expect that everything has come to your life to be beautiful in every situation.

Always feel blessed to live this life with full of goodness, happiness, richness along with self-awareness that will lead you to the greater purification of your own destiny.

Question yourself

1. Which moment showed its beauty to you?
2. What do you want to beautify in your life?

Aspiration

Being aspired to do something very important and to attain the greatest goal in your life is really a blessing. Most do not understand -

"Why do they need to aspire for their lives?"

"What is the real purpose of having an aspiration? Is it compulsory to have one?"

So great thoughts and questions arise, within each individual about what they are aspiring to do in their life and how much is it necessary?

We only come to an understanding when someone else achieves something. An aspiration can be only attained successfully only when you have a great inspiration to do so. There needs to be a great focus on what you really need to do.

It is always better if you have a clear decided thought that takes you to the next level shift of understanding your life. Slowly you can come to an understanding that when you look at something with a focus of achieving it, you will come to a full attainment of success in your life. More than the word success, it can be told that it can be achieved with pure happiness.

There are a great lot of benefits when you start to aspire to a thing very deeply because it will take you to the path of attainment in your life.

Aspiration has a different role to play. It can be totally set up to follow your desire consistently. As you aspire to attain and achieve something, you need to be first clear "What do you want to do that will satisfy you?" Don't be forced to do something that someone has achieved because it was someone's desire to attain. You can take small baby steps, one after the other to achieve something even though you are not clear on "What you really want?" It is always okay. Follow what comes in your path. Analyse whether whatever you are looking for is really needed for your life or whether you will be happy with the achievement.

In every person's life, a lot of things can take place in and around. Every little situation is inspiring people towards their commitment of work. When a human is unconsciously running back of their life, sometimes they miss their aspiration to decipher what they need.

Aspirations differ from place to place and person to person. It is like the breath of a person to live this life happily. It is just a focus point on what you really want in life. It may be mentioned as a goal, desire, achievement or some point of achievement. There lies a great difference for every human being depending upon focus on a particular requirement and they might reach to it permanently or temporarily.

But be always happy for what you aspire to do since that is a great order of doing what is required for one's own life is real aspiration.

Many, many people in this world perform particular actions for a time period to fulfill their desire. Everything you aspired will always be inspired to you because you like it, without any commitment. Have a small aspiration, to have a large goal in your life as fulfillment. But a lot of aspiration should not become a forceful action to follow daily.

Every individual must have an understanding that they need to focus on what they love to do, which in return will aspire all of you to take the next necessary step. Inspired aspiration is the easiest way to achieve what you are looking for.

Question yourself

1. Is there any aspiration in your life?
2. Is your aspiration a need or want?

Patience

"Patience is my nature and patience is my personality".

What a wonderful line to be affirmed daily. Patience has a great role to be played in our life in every aspect. Patience teaches a lot of things in one's life and is experienced firsthand. Thus it is always said "**Be Patient**".

Get along with your life patiently as there is no need for a great urgency to capture anything necessarily. Going into a life of patience always teaches a lot of things that cannot be found anywhere.

Everyone's life has great things to be thought of for oneself. You need not to hurry to get something or to achieve. Wonderful things happen when you remain patient and you can watch the type of miracles you are receiving. Many people are in a lot of urgency to do and achieve something in their life. Humans decide a time to achieve their own goal in an expected time, so that they can prove to everybody that they have made their life successful.

Real success does not come in the urgency of your wants. You need great patience to achieve something great. Because the path of patience itself will mould you, as a person you are destined to be. Patience is already given to each and every individual that they have to understand themselves and shape their own life.

When you have patience you do not need to urge or get forced to achieve something in no time. Patience always teaches you perseverance. It lets you enjoy and learn the path you have travelled to reach your goal.

The person who has great patience always receives a great boon from the universe which is much larger than their expectations. As you experience patience in your life you will start to realise that there is a great shift in your life at every step.

Try to understand the difference between patience and laziness. Patience is always waiting for something to happen in its own time, with action performed in the meantime. But laziness is not taking action towards your goal and not bothering what is happening around you.

Everything never happened in its own way until and unless the universe performed in a particular way. For some people the universe gives great support based on their karma. It will turn their life upside down in no time and action. But we do need to keep waiting for miracles to happen, keep taking necessary action required for your life improvement in what you know.

Patience brings a lot of achievements and understanding for every individual without forcing themselves to reach a destiny. For certain humans they need to have a lot of understanding to achieve the requirement because without patience when they rush to succeed at something, they would not understand - What they have created? Why have they not become successful?

Patience always tries to put you in thinking and understanding mode.

What is life?

Why should it be done?

Why are all these things happening to them?

But do need to have that patience of understanding what is going around us. Real patience gives success permanently. **Success is not victory or winning but the level they have shifted from nowhere to somewhere.**

Let's give ourselves great advice -

"Patience should always be our nature without any urgency".

Question yourself

1. What is your level of patience?
2. How do you teach yourself patience?

Sacrifice

"Every life process on this earth has some or the other form of sacrifices without any identification of winning points".

"Sacrifice", what a magnificent word! This single word covers such a lot of meaning within it. It adds a lot of credit to the word, the word that is respected and looked in high respect.

Great achievements are made only through sacrifice of one's own interest. Every sacrifice has its own meaning in its own way. Sacrifice in a different way, can be through giving up certain necessary things to achieve the higher goal.

This word sacrifice is incredible, as it transforms an individual's lives tremendously. As per one's own vision and idea, people sacrifice for their own achievement.

Every sacrifice gives boons to different types of results. Certain sacrifices are known & certain unknown. But the sacrifice made, always carry its true value. Every sacrifice would not show a winning face as expected. Each sacrifice has its own level of success. But there is nothing to mention as success, it can be achieved through one's own perseverance.

Knowingly and unknowingly, there are a lot of sacrifices which really add value to a concerned person's life in a positive manner. Many people who are concerned about their life's destiny are ready to sacrifice, at any level because they know that something big is waiting to be attained.

It would be better if a human is very conscious of the future life they want to live. As you are more conscious of your understanding that "What a sacrifice is really doing in their life? How beautiful benefit is waiting for them"?

Gracious presence in their own life at every moment will always show them the right path they have to travel. Sacrificing certain good aspects always results in a better way without picturing the result, smaller or bigger.

People make a lot of sacrifices to survive in this world. Every sacrifice should be respected and valued. Some sacrifices bring outbursts in the world and result in great pride. It depends upon the circumstance, where the sacrifice has been made and for which purpose it has been made.

It is a great suggestion to make a sacrifice for the purpose of your life. Otherwise, you would not have a purpose for your life to live. Sacrifice is not only giving up certain things in life but having a consistency in certain actions to achieve and reach something bigger.

Learn to have perseverance in sacrifice since giving up things does not bring happiness in every situation but results will be good.

Sacrifice is a great respect for each and everybody at their own level of understanding. Sometimes sacrifices burden a person's life very badly, where it seems that it has started losing its value. But it would always give great results very soon or later. Everyone on this earth does not get discouraged, with the result you see around. Because all that you see is the output of others' sacrifice.

Your sacrifice is always a special and blessed one, where you need to sacrifice on your own terms, believing that the best part of life is always waiting for you.

Question yourself

1. Should there be any sacrifice in your life?
2. Is sacrifice a gain or loss?

Judgemental

"A judged person is your reflection of your thoughts that you have displayed so many times in your mind".

Looking into people, as you imagine they would be, forming your views about others is the idea of being judgemental.

As you always made the habit to judge who all you see, meet, speak etc., you do respond in your own judgemental thoughts of a particular person you see or think.

Everyone thinks that being judgemental is a clever act of deciding, what type of people we are living together with. We don't understand that we are judging correctly or wrongly. The judgement of a particular person comes from your own views or other's opinion which you would have got influenced with. As you grow older you believe that you are good at predicting people as you get in touch with, you meet or hear and know about them.

Judging a particular person, knowing about the character and behaviour differs when you judge a person whom you have not yet met but have created opinion on other people's words.

Do you think that the way you judge people is correct?

How do you get to know about a particular person?

May it not take some time to know a person, how they respond?

You never bother how you have been responding to that response, for the opinion you received from the other person. Because it is very necessary for you to know how you are behaving with that person or you are conceptualising a particular setup in your mind.

You have to understand that a particular person's attire, talk, behaviour, and character determine a person. So, you have grown with this understanding that we need to judge a person on these aspects not even knowing if it is right or wrong.

Sometimes it turns worst when you judge a person without even seeing them. This happens when you have been influenced, by others words and without knowing and seeing, you imagine a picture of that person.

The understanding in judging a person, should be taken care of because when you are judging a character, the same person may seem good to you, while for another person they may look crazy, for the third one the worst person.

Here each person judges a single person through their own reflection in mind, they are carrying. So, we need to clearly understand that a single character will always be judging on his or her perspective that they have on that person.

For every individual it is better to stop judging a person until you have known about them completely. Don't run any opinion in your mind upon a particular person with the behaviour, attitude, status etc. It is always better to think of a person before judging because one single person reflects different characters based upon the opinion of others.

No human being displays a different attitude and character throughout their life, in order to show what type of life they are living. Sometimes a judgement goes too vague because we might have mistaken a person who is actually not so.

When you approach a particular person with a mindset of improper understanding, you may lose a person unknowingly. So be at ease in judging a person, don't reflect your thoughts as another person's character. To be on the safer side you better observe the person before you get to go with. Slow yourself and let yourself understand what the other person is.

The life of humans run totally by judgement and then it reflects the own life of a person whom you think they might be. Judge a situation or a person only when the circumstances are not great. But even these things do not happen to you when you are conscious and aware of the thoughts you have.

Question yourself

1. Are you a judgmental type?

2. Do you feel regretted when you judge someone in a wrong way?

3. Is being judgmental good or bad?

Accomplishment

"Accomplishment of enlightenment and the oneness with God's energy is the real achievement of every human life".

There are a lot of things in human life to accomplish. It can be anything from a ritual, task or habit. Mankind has accomplished a lot of things in this world, which we are experiencing in our existence.

Humans have created a lot of things to improve their style of living. We have been very intelligent in inventing and discovering so many things in this world which have made human life very easy. You are sitting in one place and you are able to travel the world virtually. We need to appreciate the older generation, who has worked so much to keep this earth an enchanting place. Humans are always in search of new things which have led them to achieve and accomplish renowned discoveries, which have made their life beautiful and amazing.

But we have also been trying to accomplish ourselves in self-discovery of our life. Still humans are struggling to know - Why are they on earth? What has made them or sent them to this earth to have this life?

Many of our gurus, ancestral elders have also been in search of their life, not their external life but the life within themselves. To know -

Who are we?
Why are we operating in this body?
What type of sources is operating within us?
Where can we find the source?

Humans are really to be appreciated for their life accomplishments, in knowing their inner consciousness that is really operating human life. We have been searching for a true life through meditation, yoga and other sought of practices which can reveal the secret of our life. Many sages, great scholars, and ancestors accomplished many tasks to rediscover our lives. Very few accomplished their searches and passed on the gained wisdom to their followers about how to accomplish their lives with consciousness and awareness.

Our inner self is the greatest teacher in this universe. Nobody can teach or give more wisdom than that. Your inner consciousness always works in your favour in assisting you to achieve and accomplish "What you really want in this life".

Every human has a very great task to accomplish where most of them have not realised it yet. And nobody knows how many rebirths humans have to take, to achieve this enlightenment with the help of their own inner self. Only karma will decide their destiny along with the **HIGHER Source's blessings**.

Even though whatever accomplishment the human race has made for the survival on this earth, it becomes very meaningless until and unless people realise and learn to reach the higher life, through the wisdom they have received from their inner self.

There cannot be a competition in the human mind to achieve enlightenment because no one can predict, when and where a person can get enlightenment and not only so they have to understand that they need to join the **Source Energy** from where they came.

Accomplishment of wisdom with the help of your source energy is the only purpose of your life. It is necessary for every human to soon realise their purpose of life and practice all the procedures and rituals to get wisdom on reaching that Source Energy as early as possible. Otherwise, no humans irrespective of their age, gender and status, will not have the ability to attain enlightenment and they would have to undergo a lot of suffering in a different birth so that they successfully achieve their purpose.

So, it is only a great request for every human life on the earth to clear up their karmas and get wisdom with God's blessings, to accomplish the life of oneness with the HIGHER Source Energy.

Unimaginable

"Better you always imagine what you really need for your life because the power of imagination can bring such a lot of things that are unimaginable".

You always imagine the things you need for life. You are creating the world you want to live and survive.

Greater things happened as you imagine in current reality without realising "What would happen in the future?" The only realisation is that you want something good to happen to you. As the imagination grows, your evolution of life also starts to happen. You will only realise your capacity of imagination only when it appears in front of you that very big and unbelievable scenes happen.

Everyone's life is created only through human imagination, without knowing the level of energy it is carrying into your life. More greatly to tell that there is a lot of unimaginable energy which creates the scenes so fast and forcefully, which you would not even expect to happen so easily.

Most of the unimaginable things are happening all around the world, without realisation through normal people's imagination. This world was designed and created by a greater Source Energy in its own imagination of perfection, realising what will be the result for the humans to survive and live a happy life. But we humans are not conscious enough to create the reality of life. People around the world have grown the imagination of life into a critical one.

In order to live, mankind thinks that they have to suffer a lot. Actually, we humans are programmed to believe that we are born to suffer and only suffering, struggling, have to be the daily part of our life. Very few realise that life runs under creative imagination through a conscious mind where they can live the life they want. All humans are superhuman but unaware of the consciousness, they are still struggling in the world, not realising that they have created their life under critical situations.

Humans have to very soon learn, how their life issues and situations are happening as well as for every person on this earth. They need to know that life is very easy and simple, if they have thought and imagined life with full of abundance and happiness. For a great portion of life, people are struggling in their lives because of critical circumstances that they don't see any way out.

"Beautiful imagination always yields beautiful life".

As you imagine your life, let it grow through all positive thoughts embracing goodness in living. You have lot of choices for a wonderful and a happy life ever after. Here only imagination comes into play, where it can bring many more respectable things for your life that you have not dreamt about.

Imaginary things start to happen when you start to keep on adding positive thoughts and good feelings in each and every moment you are living. Life will become very miraculous, as your imagination blooms very beautifully and pleasantly.

Many great people say that only imagination is the key to your happiness. Yes! It is true that the conscious imagination always brings super good things from all over the world which you would have not expected to happen. Thoughts combined with good feelings and emotions always reflect a good and prosperous life that has never been expected.

You may live in a situation of despair or unhappiness without realising the power to create your reality. So many situations appear in front of you, giving you a chance to create a better life through imagination. But humans who get hold in the life of struggle and hardship never realise, that their life can get changed beautifully.

All humans on earth are born to live a happy and prosperous life through their unimaginable imagination, which can create a new world of reality and which will make miracles happen in each and every moment of your life.

Believe in yourself, only you have the power to emit divine energy of imagination, to turn non reality into a reality.

You are the real creator of your life. Combine your energy of imagination with your soul's energy power to reflect a better future.

Limitless

"Be limitless to enjoy the unlimited life."

Being limitless is the real choice of any human being born on this earth. It is a great choice of ones being limitless. Since you have nothing to stop you from behind and block your way from nothing.

Greater things are meant to be always limitless. As you are limitless, great life force energy always flows from the divine source that can encounter any type of unimaginable blessings to you.

You are the greatest being on the earth. You need to recognise yourself gratefully, for being the existence on this earth. You have been designed to be an abundant source, where you pull all the necessary energy to manipulate your life to your favour.

There has been a large requirement for people living on this earth, which is not and cannot be satisfied when even given abundantly. People have to understand life is very beautiful and amazing when you start being in the present moment. Life is full of good surprises where you cannot compete with the real source creator.

Everything is available for everyone. There is no need to compete to gain and receive one, when there is abundance found in this universe. You must always understand the universal creator is a limitless energy, similarly you are limitless.

Very few people have known the power of being limitless as they are connected to the creator. Most people living ordinary lives struggle to sustain this beautiful life since they don't know what type of life they are living.

Most of them think that life has very little to give them. So, they have to keep on fighting, competing to grab the things that are available in front of them. Humans see only their physical existence as a by-product that is created by regular humans. They find the materialistic life, which is in physical form, to be the real availability in their lives. They don't realise or are unaware that this universe is limitless and it has everything for everyone.

We humans don't need to keep searching and running back of our requirements, as you are really connected to the universal energy, where everything straight away flows to your hand even without your realisation.

The universe is such a big giver and it never says no to anything. Whatever we ask, it is given. Only we humans have to decide that our boon should be good or bad. Since we are the co-creator of our life process, our thoughts generate our life's requirements at every single moment of our life. But we have to generate very carefully, with full awareness of what we really do require. Because the universe does not know good or bad but only knows only to give. So, keeping this in mind, you better be aware of your thoughts each and every moment. Don't go by the artificial emotions and thoughts that are chasing you throughout your lifetime because it is not the real one that you are actually living in. Humans always live a life of unwanted fears, struggle, anger and many other emotions that never took them to the next level of life but caged them into a life of prisoner which is meant to suffer.

So, it is better that every human comes to this greater reality of consciousness that life is always limitless for each and every human born on this earth. There is a large unfinished availability of money, abundance, power, ideas, or anything you wish to have. Don't keep your mind in a limited belief or else you would not be able to escape this karmic life.

Impossible

"Raise your belief system of possibility to show the impossible result".

Anything can be possible in this world and nothing can be stopped. Everything has a possibility for attainment in this universe. Because everything in this life is brought into the reality that was once an impossible thought.

You humans have made such a lot of possibilities to happen in this life by not believing the impossible belief. Everybody knows that every human has that force energy to create anything that is apart from our imagination.

There is no such thing as impossible because this world always creates resistance, when the mindset is between creation and attainment. Don't approach anything from the idea of impossibility because the beginning of a creation itself is being stopped.

As you always approach the possibility of ways to create a new thing in your life, it always turns into one more beautiful dimensional opportunity. The opportunities further, when taken action, create marvellous results.

Only always depend on the possibilities, even if your mind does not believe it. Since our mind collapses when we try to do new things, we need not to stop our creation, and do not believe that it is not possible.

Making something possible is only in our mind, we have to make it believe that any idea, view or intention is really possible. To make a belief possible you need to have a whole idea or steps to a successful journey. It is only your mindset that believes that it accepts your ideas and intentions. When our intentions and desires are really believed without creating any resistance as a second thought, our manifestations happen easily as we always want them.

You must carry a strong belief that everything in this world is always possible. Don't concentrate on difficulties or problems to make your life more complicated since this life revolves on the possibility of survival. When you get to know and understand that life has a lot of openings in all the best ways but our mind chatter does not let us make life beautiful since it is caught between possibility and impossibility.

As much as possible prepare yourself for all the good things that are available for you without any resistance. As you come to know and understand that life is full of possibilities combined with opportunities, you will actually realise that you have started to create a beautiful life which in return will give you the best life you want to live. Understand the desires that arise, have real good intentions and try to take forward with the mantra **"Everything is Possible"**.

As your belief is built very strongly around the intention you had, it will start to create a beautiful picture of reality. This belief in the possibility of making things happen step by step will result in a great opening of achievability. The stages of achievability are made possible when your belief system has grown stronger and stronger because you will start to see and receive all the unimaginable things.

The return of interest for the belief of possibilities and unimaginable creation makes everything tremendous for you. You have all the mental strength within you, which lets you in the creation of your world.

"Never underestimate the power of your mind very easily since it has a great equation of moving things from impossible to possible".

Only you have the real power for your life's creation with a strong belief of understanding as how the mind is working. When you truly come to understand that your belief must be very strong even without knowing the result. Belief makes things possible but before making anything possible for you understand what is really needed in your life because this world always needs good creation for all the beautiful lives to survive on earth.

Self-Esteem

"Your self-esteem is the reflection of your self-value to oneself".

Are you conscious of what is happening to you and happening within you? Actually, it never happens to everyone until a person is in awareness.

Okay, what is the need of self-esteem for a person? Is it actually needed? Everyone always tries to show and behave with some respect to other people in a situation. Since we are all well-known and also trained to show respect to the people who are with us or even to unknown people. But why not be educated, taught by anyone that self-esteem is really very important for every person's growth internally and personally. Because people never learn to value themselves and do not feel the importance of respecting oneself. Here respecting oneself is not a bigger work or the process to be followed but it is a must follow regularity to handle oneself with respect.

Do I have to daily follow and practice self-esteem? Yes! It is to be done not in practice but it has to be your regular character. Your self-esteem is a very important part of life and shows how important you are for yourself.

You can make sacrifices or adjustments in your life by not hurting your self-esteem because you are the most unique person for yourself and your soul does require its own respect and love in the form of self-esteem.

Most humans do not consider their self-esteem when striving to win a situation or when hoping for circumstances to become favourable for them. You individuals do not understand how valuable you are, when you are losing your self-esteem.

"You are the born diamond with divine energy that purely serves on true respect, love, happiness and peace".

As you never valued your life, you will never know how self-esteem is hurting your inner soul. You can struggle, suffer in many situations in your life, but never underestimate that you are not valuable.

Self-esteem consciousness sometimes creates a very big problem also. Since humans do not know whether they are fighting for their self- esteem or ego, because ego and self- esteem both go hand in hand only with small differences. You really need to know whether you are solving a situation through ego or self-esteem. Your ego always tries to win the situation by putting the opposite person down but self-esteem does not so, it will demand self-respect even though the situation is very tough. As you gradually know how to define self- esteem, you will start to feel more comfortable in any type of situation by not letting yourself down.

Self-esteem always plays a very beautiful game, where most people always mistake it for ego, whatever it may be never try to lose your self-esteem for anyone. Since nothing is unique in this world other than you.

Embrace your self-esteem very beautifully and patiently because your self-esteem will surely take you to a very great height, when managed properly.

It is better we educate all the generations around us that self-esteem is a very important thing, to be always connected with an inner soul. When the inner soul is always connected, then this world becomes a happy place to live.

Grow your self-esteem slowly by not hurting yourself. Self-esteem is a very beautiful act of love and respect towards you, where it does not require any external validation.

Embarrassing

Life is full of incidents and situations causing good and embarrassing moments. We are most of the time held up in a situation without even knowing, why is it just happening?

Life has to keep going in its flow, to capture the moments with different emotions. You are always held in the situation of over thinking, what will happen to you? Not knowing that everything is happening for a reason.

We humans as born on this earth planet tend to believe that life is only full of difficulties. Only lucky and rich people live the life they want. But it usually does not work in this way, since life is full of assumptions without knowing what is happening.

Greatly, we also tend to believe that life is full of choices whether to live a happy or unhappy life. Life always takes us to different directions depending upon the thoughts that we acquire in a particular situation. If something good is always happening, we believe that it is good, if not, our decision is wrong. So, what is the connection to being embarrassed in a situation?

There are a lot of places where we face a lot of embarrassing moments. It might be due to unawareness of what is happening around us. Many embarrassing moments come in life to make you understand how well you have handled yourself.

Yes, when you know how to handle any type of situation, you get to realise that there is no situation of embarrassment. Because when you know yourself very well, you realise that there is no need for any external validation, as nothing hurts you.

You being a consciously aware person, you never get hurt or embarrassed easily in any situation. The embarrassing situation only exists in that moment, when it does not go your way. Expected and unexpected situation, sometimes lead to embarrassing moments, but a realised person takes no situation for granted and does not allow anything to cause embarrassment.

You better understand that any embarrassing moment, was only created by you. Your unconscious mind has picked these types of moments to reflect in your life. You might sometimes see that one particular person will be getting stuck in an embarrassing situation often, it is due to the actions and their thoughts that they performed earlier.

Some feel very embarrassed for what they are, because they are not able to escape their life's situation. Embarrassing situations might often come to you, when you always keep on comparing yourself with others. You feel all the situations are embarrassing for you because you're always compared to yourself.

Being you is a great thing, to live a happy life for yourself. But you think that people are always embarrassing you for being yourself. It is actually true because people around us believe that we have to live up to other people's expectations and requirements. The society around us stands against us for being real, be it your own family or the people around you. Even though the situation is so bad, learn to act a bit to suppress the embarrassing situation. As you know this world only survives on dramas, untruthfulness and unworthy things as people think it is real.

"You born as human always get to know about yourself only the way you handle your situation whether it is embarrassing or not."

Even though the external situation is embarrassing for you in any case, you need not bring that situation to your inner reality. Because your inner self does not deserve all those things, that are really happening externally.

Silence

" Silence blooms the flower of consciousness through different layers of awareness".

Whatever you do and whatever you perform, there exists some silence in that action. It is meant to be that from silence only an action appears. When you rest yourself, you literally get a chance to take action, since your mind tells you what to do. As you realise there is some sort of communication existing between your silence and action.

Silence is a very great word, with a very strong power that can be felt when you live in that silence. This silence teaches you a lot of lessons which words cannot teach. We get so many opportunities to express ourselves through words and actions, but silence tends to have much more powerful density in its own way.

We mostly think that silence is to stay calm or not to speak to anybody. But actual silence is not that it is an actionless, wordless answer with a strong voice. Silence cannot be heard or seen by the normal way. It is an actual action of nothingness, full of meaning and answers for all the questions you have in your head.

You can experience silence for yourself or when somebody stays in silence. It is a very slow expression but a very strong answer, where you would feel that everything is finished.

Our great gurus and ancestors voluntarily practiced silence in their own way. They actually knew the power of being in silence. Silence has taught a large lesson of untold stories, which is meant to be understood only while you learn it.

Real silence is not keeping quiet or not communicating with anybody. It is the silence of your mind, keeping your mind in control or trying to slow down the thoughts of your mind.

Every great guru, spiritual leaders of any religion had a habit of staying in silence at regular intervals. The silence gave them immense pleasure in understanding their life, where words could not explain it.

"Silence is a powerful tool to enhance the power of everything in this world. Nowhere, nothing other than silence is so vibrant to reach you, the real consciousness".

SILENCE means consciousness

SILENCE means universe

SILENCE means God

Silence is everything in this expanded consciousness, none other than this the universe evolves. **Silence your mind, you will be enlightened**. It is the greatest tool to get enlightened. Many of the gurus knew its power and practice still today.

It is such a great experience when you put yourself in silence. Silence gives you all the answers that you are searching for in your life restlessly. You are the silence as the soul has to be and meant to be.

Your soul loves silence because it knows the power of silence. When you stay in silence your questions are answered very easily. Your mind brings all the things which you need in life through silence.

Understanding the internal silence brings all the answers from the external physical world. You might be astonished how these things are happening. There is nothing different, everything external is also internal in existence, but we are not able to see since there is no awareness. Silence has great stories to tell you about the reality of your life.

"You do not get an answer when you question, but you are answered only when you are in silence".

Possessiveness

"Don't become possessed by possessiveness by losing all the beautiful attributes which are needed in this life".

Possessiveness is a very great topic of extreme attachment and owning anything without any condition.

So, as we use the word possessiveness externally, it looks that a person is too attached or having more love for something. But actually, it is not so. It is a very deep connection without any reason and having a great feeling towards ownership.

Being possessive in a relationship sometimes feels very good. Many times, it is like a parrot in a golden cage not letting the person do anything.

Okay! When we get attached to something more than really needed, it can be considered to be possessive in nature. But we humans born on this earth have become possessive of everything, let it be humans, animals and worldly materialistic life.

Are not we too attached to this materialistic life? We think it is really necessary, but not knowing why we stick to everything, from relationships to material and money. Since we think that we own it and we have the right to do it.

Humans earlier had a common thought that everything in this world was to be shared and used equally. But as the humans started becoming more and more unrealistic, they started to become more possessive of each and everything in this life. As we got attached, we started facing a lot of problems. Since we think that **"I have the right to own it and have it"**. Humans have not found it easy to give up on anything they own. Not understanding that everything in this world is only an illusion. This illusion has created everything both living and non-living things as we perceive them. But in reality to express, there is nothing like living and non-living thing, here in this universe everything is energy, vibrating in different frequencies.

Now when we know that everything is illusion and everything is energy, then what is there to become possessive of? You have nothing to hold on to yourself. Your personal life is holding the largest source of illusion.

"Your possessiveness itself is an illusion holding your life apart from reality".

Many people have no consciousness of their understanding. Why is life designed in this way? Why has everything become an illusion? And no humans are ready to accept reality.

Only certain awake and enlightened people understand that the life they live is full of illusion and imagination. Nothing is real and nothing is unreal.

The world has a very large meaning to make you understand that the more you are possessive and attached the more it is difficult for you to move to the next dimension of your life.

Most of the humans get locked with this attachment, believing this is the reality. When you are too attached to this worldly life, you will have great anxiety and stress to live life on this earth. Since you think that you have no ability to survive without this relationship and materialistic life.

When you are aware, get detached from this materialistic life. For you, life becomes easy and joyful. More possessiveness always takes to more struggle and suffering, not knowing how to survive without this possessiveness.

Learn to detach yourself little by little we do not want you to get away from everything once for all. But I need you to understand that, this is the reality of life that nothing in this world including you and me is real. When you and me itself is not real then what could make you so possessive to get attached to this materialistic life?

As your possessiveness increases, do understand that there is disappearance of love, joy, happiness, freedom and many more things that are actually needed for you to survive on this planet.

Don't lose your survival sources without any love, joy & happiness, because there is no other purpose to live on this earth. Be cautious and careful as early as possible, get out of the string of possessiveness.

Prejudice

"Prejudice is the story writer of your life, of happiness and suffering."

Prejudice is the name of faultiness, unawareness and misunderstanding of right things. All fall into the prey of prejudice without our consciousness since we think that we are good at taking decisions properly. Lack of proper understanding puts you into an unwanted situation where you don't realise what type of prejudice you have created around yourself.

This word prejudice has a great play in every person's life knowingly and unknowingly. You never understand the situation, when you prejudice a circumstance. Actually, we people easily judge things effortlessly without knowing what has happened. We sometimes get hold as prejudiced victims, unconsciously in a repeated process.

People's lives are full of ups and downs where prejudice plays a very great role. Most of the time a lot of importance is given in the name of prejudice, depending on a feeling, emotion and action.

In order to solve a particular problem or resolve a circumstance, we in urgency tend to take prejudiced decisions, not knowing that later its effect will be affecting our life to a greater extent.

A human who is not aware or conscious of one's own thoughts will easily fall into the cage of prejudice. Because human nature always lives in great emotions and feelings, these emotions play a very great role in creating your life. But very few are considerate about the type of situation they are living in and why such circumstances repeatedly occur in their life.

> *"People belonging to the religion of consciousness and awareness are the great builders of life Empire."*

The person with more awareness tries to put life at ease. When you slow down your mind with full clarity, the appearance of prejudice in the areas of life starts diminishing, you understand that life has less misery but a lot of happiness.

Humans who live in this critical life always feel that they are major sufferers and they are always punished for merely existing. This mankind which is entangled in this karmic debt never comes out at all. Since these karmic debts never let any human escape this life of suffering easily, because humans are born to dissolve their karmas that they carried to this earth, and they must experience all good and bad karmas without any escapism.

A prejudiced decision or activity has a greater effect on every area of life. Because it creates so many problems and sufferings unnecessarily, without knowing what they are suffering for with all these things. It happens due to being unconsciously victimized by your life and a lack of awareness.

An individual nested inside the victim's consciousness due to prejudice really falls into the prey of suffering and disaster not knowing what to do with their life and how to survive this life happily.

So, as you face a situation or any critical circumstance, it is better for every human to slow down before creating any scene next. Since humans have also understood the prejudice effects caused to themselves and people around them.

"If you have to live a life of betterment of victim -free survival, consciousness and awareness are the only medicine to be applied".

Prejudice is the birth of all problems and all sorts of unexpected situations in each individual's life. Know yourself first, be careful with what you understand and know. Analyse everything you are dealing with in life and strive to create a situation that provides freedom from suffering and isolation. Be cautious at each and every step of your life before you blame others and yourself.

Enthusiasm

"Being an enthusiast or being with an enthusiast, there is growth in life with a lot of consciousness".

Be an Enthusiast

Being an enthusiast or being in enthusiasm always is the greatest gift you will ever have. There comes a great advantage in life when you become more enthusiastic. Since when you start feeling better about being yourself or feeling more active about you, it adds a great bonding of goodness and wonderfulness in your life.

Surely there would be a great event of wonderful things that would start happening within you. You would feel more confident, rich and prosperous when your enthusiasm starts rising. You need not think anything bad since your enthusiastic behaviour will always put you in the next level of stage, where you will be carried to the higher state of life. In this way, unimagined and unthinkable things start appearing before you and life would become more miraculous.

"Everything you desire with great enthusiasm always will reach the path of goodness which takes you to the path of success and fame".

We can find a lot of interest in this lifetime among those who have been doing a lot of good things which they love.

Mostly, these enthusiastic people are very thrilling people to be with because these people always know that their life is meant for them. They never try to impress anybody. They always go and live by the inner self desire, which always guides them in the righteous path of success.

There never arises any fear when you would become a great enthusiast, since you live only on your own desire and belief. And always take care to see that you are happy with what you are doing.

Enthusiasts never fear facing failure because they know that there is a powerful guidance, which will always think only for their goodness. And these types of people always keep moving to the next step and never stop even if they find any obstacle standing in their way.

As soon as you reach a certain level of success, some enthusiasts just drop down from that level of life. Again, they work themselves from the beginning, to build themselves. As much as possible, you should put yourself into the shoes of enthusiasm and it will take you to the greatest level of achievement. More enthusiastic means more goodness in life.

Life is like a wave which rises and slows down automatically without any reason. But an enthusiast will always see it as a silent and peaceful river. Try to put yourself as much as possible into opportunities of life, where you will be getting the next step to move towards your desire.

As you try to live the life you want to live, just add love to it. Next step will be carried by your inner self who knows better than you. It will take you to the path of awareness with righteousness.

Being in the level of enthusiasm is the greatest gift in life. Don't miss it, since every winner and loser always has something to say about themselves to the world.

Empowerment

Power yourself with knowledge and the idea of becoming stronger to create difference from others. It is not only to stay stronger but to believe in yourself, the power you hold to ignite the fire inside you.

You people generally think empowerment is freedom or getting help from somebody to improve your life. Actually, the real empowerment comes from within you, it is an arousal of one self.

To be explained, it is a kind of awareness you gently realise about yourself and understand consciously, that something powerful is working on behalf of us to make life better.

Empowerment is the real experience you have within yourself when a great situation arises. Each and everyone have to undergo the situation wherever possible because it shows the real power that is hiding inside you. You can find within yourself through great realisation, when you turn your focus within you. This big YOU inside yourself bring all the knowledge, wisdom, power and requirements that is really needed for you. It really knows what you are up to and what you really need.

Being more conscious and aware you will enjoy your real power that you were unaware of. The greatest mode of life is knowing who you are.

Wow! It would be a very great feeling for the authority you possess within yourself but nobody has any right to destroy it. It is the value which is hidden inside, waiting for a time to show up its tremendous power of realisation that **"How powerful you are?"**

You get empowered each and every time, when a real situation triggers. You do have to know, that you do not need to externally search for help to empower you. This empowerment is not an external factor to search and get help from it.

It actually lies within you. It is always present within you. When you are really in need or struggling to get out of a situation, you have compelled energy, which is trying to burst out and is willing to help you.

Clear awareness and patience help you to access empowerment that is lying within yourself. It may not be physical but an unknown factor, which is so powerful that tries to make you understand and feel that there is no requirement for any external energy to aid you.

Empower your feelings and thoughts with the source energy - the greatest universal empowerment. Where you don't understand, what makes you feel so powerful and empowered.

Feel great to be empowered at every moment of your life since it is that Divine Energy protecting you, guiding and always taking care of you.

Greatness

"You are the real greatness living in the human form. Don't research and waste your life to show your greatness. Everything will come out tremendously when your soul shines out unimaginably".

Everything in this world exists in the greatness of God. We need no assurance in the creativity of God existing in front of us. All the wonderfulness that we are experiencing is only in the creation of the highest source **GOD**.

Great events always have their occurrence in their own way. It reflects in such a marvellous picture where you feel something extraordinary has been showcased. Everything in this world, right from the creation to the last event of exhaustion, has its own greatness.

Good times are always put in front of us, to first understand the greatness of ourselves. We humans forget to appreciate the capability of our own creation and never trust the greatness of what we have created.

More and more experiences are received from knowledge and wisdom, the way humans have educated themselves reveals the real greatness of their life. God's creation is always in the bombardment of the reality of what we are expecting. It is great beyond our thoughts and imagination. In the similar way the human creation is in its own bombardment one after the other. Even the human mind is not smaller than anything. There always exists a divine essence in every human born on this earth. The divine essence plays a very great role even without consciousness and awareness. It knows how to bring out the greatness of each individual's life that is to be showcased on this earth.

Greatness can be the fame or anything that holds a high value. But our Highest Source Energy works to manifest nothing beyond the reality of our soul particle. It brings out the real purpose of greatness that has come to be displayed on this earth. Every soul has its own purpose to perform its greatness by serving people in different forms and varieties.

Actually, the important thing is that we need to understand that greatness always exists within us. You need to search or develop certain things to attain greatness. Everything you do on this earth plain is real greatness.

You have not come here to suffer or struggle to survive on this earth but you have been presented in this earth to show yourself the purpose you are born with, the real greatness that already exists within yourself. It is well assured that each and every soul always shines in its own greatness. Hence you need not work very hard to bring out your greatness. It is actually a natural process which has been embedded within us.

The wholesome greatness of human life is that there is always the existence of goodness in our life's journey. No humans need not doubt themselves whether they are capable or not. Everyone is the greatest achiever of their own existence on this earth. As we acquire the knowledge of consciousness and awareness, the fuel of greatness rises very powerfully and shoots right into the universe, where reaching a point is not decidable.

Certainty

There is no certainty of anything on this earth. No one can give you a permanent assurance of existence in this world. Everything in this world has its own level of existence for a particular time period, but nothing can have its permanent existence. Whatever you see, believe and feel has certainty only for a particular period of time. Here time is not defined according to universal law. The life of humans has no certainty, along with other creations in this world. This life of existence for everything, as we assume does not really exist forever. When life has no certainty we humans are still struggling very hard to sustain this life as much as possible.

There is no need to get frightened of life, where there is no assurance. Since everything in this world comes and goes. To be explained clearly one form of reality dissolves into the other form of reality.

We humans create a lot of things in this world every moment from time to time, to fulfill our needs and requirements. But we do not understand that creation of anything is changing itself at one stage of time. We think that everything stays in this world permanently, but it is not so.

This world is an illusion of physical state, we have to realise that the reality of known is already an illusion then how come what we have created and believed to be, will have any certainty.

The world creation in this universe has its own creation under the name of illusion, which cannot be largely realised by the human mind. It is actually far from human understanding. The assurance of any physical or nonphysical existence cannot be defined to be definite. Since in the actual realisation there is no certainty of any creation. It has its own form of reality as we assume.

We do not need to get confused in this theory of certainty because it does not provide any guarantee of real existence.

You presume these events, incidents, situations or any form of circumstances as the reality of existence for the human to survive in a particular situation. But here nothing is real and there is no certainty of any state of life.

Thus it would be better if every human realises the existence on this earth and unearths their life's purpose of survival. When you get to know your birth on this earth has no certainty for the struggle you're going through to live. You will realise this uncertainty of life and feel no struggle or suffering which has any real meaning. And it is only a part of your karma. Assumption of life process, living in a certain limit of your life has nothing to do about any survival on this earth.

Question yourself

   1. Have you experienced any certainty in your life?

Unsuccessful

"The real success lies only in the mind of a really fulfilled person".

Is there anything to be said as success and no success? Humans have defined the definition for success. And everyone on this earth lives by these definitions. Yes! It is true we assume everything in life has to travel the path of success or failure.

To prove yourself to this world you need to perform something or the other that results either in success or not being successful. Ok, we believe the people who are successful or have been successful are meant to be appreciated, valued and respected. Because humans have developed the theory that only successful people, such as people with highest status, money, fame are meant to be successful.

Are we very sure that these are the real successful people on this earth? What happens to the people who have not achieved anything that the society is looking for? Every human in the society is labelled with the name of success. Nobody realises that real success is not money or fame but it is actually survival on this earth each and every day with being full of gratitude and happiness.

"Live life of happiness in each and every moment of your breath as it flows in and comes out - the REAL SUCCESS EXIST HERE."

Here every part of life of the humans is differentiated in categories according to human assumptions. Mankind believes that every human born on this earth has to be successful in whatever they do, as well as they have to prove themselves to the society that they are the winner of a particular job they do. Otherwise, we humans do not respect them.

Actually, all humans believe strongly that we are born to show success to other people around us and want to carry the ego of success on our head still we exist on this earth. Very few humans have realised that life does not lie between being successful and unsuccessful, not good or bad. But our life only exists between the karmas of good and bad actions.

Day by day we come across many unsuccessful people. But actually, we should not label them. They might not seem to be successful for others, but they might be successful parents, breadwinners, savers, etc. Every human is making their life successful in their own personal way. We live in a very large community of humans, who live their life to their ability in order to make their families, friends, career and many other things successful and which satisfies their life each and every day.

Dear people don't really go for any acknowledgement in the name of success. You are the divine being suffering unnecessarily without knowing the reality that you have come to live this life happily and help the people around you.

It is better you do not need to prove anything to anyone. Live your life happily as your inner soul guides you. Your inner soul is the thing that is always looking at oneness with you apart from you being a success or failure. Your real soul never looks how you are and how you perform. It wants only one thing - happiness in your life.

Be in present moment of this life each and every second and success will be yours.

The road map to SUCCESS -

"Love your LIFE. Be in HAPPINESS. Live this MOMENT - YOU ARE SUCCESSFUL."

Question yourself

1. Do you experience unsuccessfulness in your life?
2. What is unsuccessful meant to you?

Powerfulness

"Just believe the power (SOUL) in you. Your every step and action will be showcased powerfully to this world."

Being in the power & feeling the power is the greatest blessing in life. When you can feel the power very strongly, you can understand how truly powerful you are.

Yes! Life has always something to give us in some or the other way, which has always been needed in your life. You had always longed to receive something in life. In reality you have always received, what you have been longing for. Now you understand how powerful you are because you have received what you had always thought of.

So, where does this power lie in you? The powerful feelings that you search within, only arise from your inner self. You need not create any power within yourself because the real one already exists inside you and only needs to be triggered by your sense of connection.

How to invoke the power within yourself? Just try to connect yourself deeply rather than correcting an external circumstance, factor or anything else that is always bothering you a lot. When you truly get connected to your inner self, in a peaceful mind you will understand the amount of power you have been holding throughout unknowingly. There is nothing to tell, it's only due to unawareness and unconsciousness that never let you meet your powerful inner self.

The biggest powerful switch of your life is the "SOUL" - residing silently, but which is powerful.

As you and your soul build a strong connection you do not need any external factor to set up your life in a proper way. Because the instrument that holds within yourself knows better than anybody, what you really need in this life span. So better trust this power factor- **SOUL,** the ruler of everything and divine inside, which is ready to start miracles for you in order to set your life properly.

You do not need to struggle or suffer to reach or get connected to your soul. The easiest way is just being silent in your mind - stop mind chatter and be peaceful. Once you learn to be conscious and aware, the divine soul connection can be felt, which is always speaking to you, from the first day of your birth, to the last day of your life.

When you gradually start feeling and hearing the **SOUL** talk, you will be amazed and realise, that you actually have nothing to think or do. Your **SOUL** always has the full freedom to manipulate your life, always in the best way. Just listen to it, how beautifully it keeps on instructing and helping you about what to do and what not to do.

As your understanding with the inner self gets deeper, life will become so miraculous, that you need not put any mental effort to make your life good.

Just listen to your inner self and take action accordingly. You will just start seeing how beautiful your life has changed without any struggle.

So now, you would understand that, everything that is given in your life is very powerful and that they are only meant for you. Your **SOUL** knows what is really needed for you.

Now I believe the affirmation is really justified -

"I AM POWERFUL (SOUL)".

Question yourself

1. What is the power inside you telling now?
2. Define your powerful experience?

Uniqueness

"Your uniqueness is how different you are enabled in very different ways that others don't possess in the same way you do".

Finding yourself to be unique is such an ideal thing in life. If you need to be different, you need to have it. Actually, all humans have their own uniqueness without ever realising themselves. Everyone believes that uniqueness is a victory. But it is not at all and there is nothing to do with victory and success.

So, let's specify that, do you need to showcase your ideas or uniqueness to this world all the time. It is not necessary because you are born with a unique nature of yourself which you do not realise. We all believe that we are just born similar. Yes, it is true but the nature and the purpose of life does not support or reflect any other person in this world as you. You are not even a replica of anything that exists on this earth.

Every living and non-living thing has a special uniqueness in its own way. Where we would not find any difference in any one until the uniqueness unknowingly reflect on us. Everybody and nobody are the same on the earth.

Better realise the uniqueness of yourself because we all carry different souls. Everything has its own performance power, for the body it is residing in. Like many other people, most even try to understand their special uniqueness, which actually will make them unique in the crowd.

Here uniqueness can be anything like character, behaviour or anything that shows the power surprisingly. Many do not realise the inner power they are holding inside. It actually comes out when it is needed. When you really identify consciously, it becomes a part of your life and becomes reality.

Everyone on this earth is blessed with their own uniqueness of the soul. Do always understand that every soul is powerful and divine. It has unbelievable power in such a way that the body it carries which connects from birth to death, always performs conscious actions in order to make that particular life reach the path of enlightenment.

One must understand very clearly that you and other humans born on this earth have no other work other than bringing love and compassion on this earth and surviving on it. You have only come to have it and attain it.

Love and compassion are the only paths where you can get enlightened and reach the **Highest Source Energy** which is in the form of light. So, when you understand all these things, you should come to a high conclusion that every angle of life is only built and meant for the purpose of your enlightenment. There is nothing more than this on this earth to achieve.

Even though you have other responsibilities to perform, using your uniqueness, try to get aware and conscious to climb the ladder of enlightenment.

Your uniqueness is your actual enlightenment. Actually, when you realise **"WHO AM I?"** & **"WHAT AM I?"** this shows the power of your uniqueness. The way you have understood to choose to identify yourself is what that uniqueness is working within you in order to achieve the higher energy source.

Question yourself

1. Do you believe that you are a unique being?
2. How do you identify your uniqueness?

Divineness

"Divineness is a great feeling of blissful emotion that lets you to lift the life to greatness".

Finding divineness within you is such a good thing. There always exists divineness in every action you do. You are the greatest being in yourself. Everything in you and around is divine in its own form. Great things are not to be considered as divine because each single thing that has bloomed and is provided on this earth carries its own divineness.

A very large number of people believe that divinity always exists in a particular place, situation or matter which is popularly believed. Actually, it is not so, the divinity sense of understanding, falls apart with most of humans.

You need to understand that every creation has its divineness because you are created by the divine energy and you are a part of it also. You and everything in this world is embedded with divineness. There is no form of shape or size to identify the divineness within anything.

Divineness is the feeling you sense and receive from a particular action, situation or anything. There is no definite thing to describe the divine form of what you feel.

In a lifetime every person has experienced a lot of divineness in every situation of life. Divineness can be any form of greatness, goodness, beauty or expressiveness. When you get in contact with it and feel the energy of happiness and goodness, you understand how divine it is.

The people are all blessed with their own divine nature, not only humans, every creature or every other thing is full of divineness. It is not showcased in any particular way.

Everyone's divineness is in the form of energy or GOD's power, it reflects in a different form in a different nature and in every different situation. So, to be precise there is divinity in everything you do.

Don't you humans understand that you are not a human, actually you are a divine soul dressed as human to survive on this earth. Whatever the situation might be, divineness is always showing up in each and every human and situation to situation.

What a beautiful and lucky human we are since we have been carrying GOD within each one of us. Our **GOD - SOUL** is always speaking to us and is always there in any situation, showing love, compassion and happiness during all the times.

Every being on this earth is a gifted one, which is unknown to us because we sustain and live our life depending on the external factors. These external factors always keep triggering us to a great extent. We humans get caught hold inside this mechanics and materialistic life system and struggle to come out believing that this is the way we have to live. And we are also unaware that there is a great divine power existing within each one of us, which is waiting to help us throughout our lifetime without any condition. So to understand -

> *"Divineness is the shine with which you glitter, is installed like a diamond. Bring your diamond out to sparkle and give light to this world".*

Question yourself

1. You and your divineness?
2. How beautiful is your divineness?

Faithfulness

Some people have a tendency to always have trust in things that are always comfortable to their belief. These people do not analyse whether it is good or bad, needed or not needed in their life. Anything that triggers people's emotions and brings fear about their life becomes a strong belief system. Most of the time humans fear that something will happen to them, if they do not believe. We tend to support the circumstances that are always not in our comfort zone. It is due to the fear they accept that belief not understanding, if it is applicable to the life situation or not. So far human life has been growing from the autosuggestion of some other people's beliefs. Do understand that people have different situations and every person does not come from the same background. So everyone's perspective of life changes time to time.

Okay, then what to believe and what not? You should be aware and conscious of what's happening in your life at every moment because every life situation runs with its own belief system, which has formed consciously through your awareness.

Why do we humans tend to believe whatever they see, hear and feel? Since generations to generations our exposure to the society has been developed only on a certain belief system. But have we explored that all the beliefs we had carried so far are realistic and really needed in our lives? Never have we put any effort into our life system, as it has been moving throughout our lifetime.

We are always living in a fake, unrealistic life not understanding what to believe and what not. Who will teach us? What is real, in this unrealistic life? Only our soul can help us and tell the truth about our life. Without our inner guidance you would not be able to differentiate life's reality. Through conscious awareness, we will learn to realise the reality that is happening within us. But to know what is really needed and not needed in life - your faith comes into being.

Okay, what does faithfulness have to do here? Yes, a question rises in our mind. But our faithfulness to our inner soul makes us understand, what life is and why are we born on this earth? Every understanding in life always comes to you, only when you are faithful to your inner self.

Faithfulness tends to surrender to your inner self, understanding that it will take care of everything in your life. When your faith grows on your inner self, you and your soul get connected and become a whole system of awareness.

The whole consciousness makes you aware of what life system you're about to live and what type of belief system you have to follow. As you slowly increase your faith in your soul all the doors of opportunity start opening one after another. Finally at one point of time you understand how far your belief system is deepened and how you are forced to live this illusion life.

The actual belief system is full of misery and imperfection, not letting any humans realise that in their lifetime they suffer only because of the untamed belief system, which has grown all these years, is actually fake and influenced by other people.

You have been suffering only due to the unfaithful behaviour on your own. Here, your self is none other than your soul. When your unfaithfulness increases from every direction of life you get held with fear, suffering and guilt. So finally, what you realise is that your faithfulness has increased life, happiness and goodness that now tends to flow in your life because only you know what is needed for your life. Your inner self gets triggered and awakens when only faithfulness becomes stronger.

Being faithful to your life system is a general term of happiness and blissfulness, so be it that way.

Question yourself

1. How faithful you are to your life?

Blissfulness

"Blissful - Being Enlightened - the very highest stage of life achievement for which purpose you have to live, realise, and dissolve yourself within your inner self".

Being yourself is the greatest bliss one can have in life. Everything and everybody do not get to have a state of blissfulness, when you are not being in a self mode. To be so, it takes a lot of awareness and consciousness in combination to enjoy blissfulness in each and every moment of life. So, it is very necessary for each and every individual born on this earth to attempt to live their life the way they want to be.

We living in a greater community of relationships are not allowed to be thyself. Yes! We have always been compelled to live for others' wishes, thinking that we are sacrificing ourselves, to see happiness in other people's lives. But do not realise how much damage we have caused to ourselves. There is nothing to blame yourself since we have no idea of what type of life we are living because we have not been taught how to see and understand our lives. Most of our ancestors did not possess the knowledge and idea. Actually they didn't know neither -"Why are we living this life?" or "What is the purpose of people living this life with different lifestyles?" or "Why are some happy and why are some very sad?" Many did not have the teachings and realisation "How to live our life?" Really they did not know.

Who has gained wisdom to teach us how to live this life blissfully? Not many and many of us do not even think that it is easy to live life blissfully and is it necessary to live so. Dear humans do understand we are actually really meant only to live in happiness and blissfulness "But how?"

There is always an answer to the questions asked. Similarly, to be blissful, first live your life happily at each and every stage in your life. Actually, to be more precise, look into every moment of your life. See how much each and every moment is favouring your life and making your life meaningful. This only happens when you learn to live in the present moment. Next question arises "How?" and "Is it possible to live in the present moment?"

Yes! Surely it is very much possible and there are many ways you can be so, but it can happen only when you believe that you can transform your life easily and intentionally. You have nothing to do with the past or future because the past is done and the future is yet to come. Only thing left to ask is the present moment, which has a lot of power within itself when you get along with it.

Lot of creativity and ideas arise only when you are in the present moment. World creation and materialistic life was also created only when you were in the present moment. Life always starts with the present moment, which brings real happiness in life.

You might wonder why I am telling you to be in the present moment since it gives you a lot of awareness about your life and the birth of creation happens in this present moment. As you get addicted to living in the present moment your life becomes more blissful than accepted because you do not have to worry and think about the past and future of your life.

As you start living blissfully, everything is easily possible for you without any struggle. This blissfulness always lets you come out of guilt and fear. You will become least bothered about others status, lifestyle and relationship.

Blissfulness is a blessed life, for one who knows how to live this life. Try being yourself in this present moment and every moment. Live for your happiness not for disturbing or bothering others life. Always know that blissfulness is a gift from the higher self. The one, who has become an expert in being blissful, is the blessed child of the universe - chosen Enlightened Soul. Everyone take guidance from their inner self, the only being that knows the solution for every problem.

Question yourself

1. Do you have any option to be blissful?
2. Have you gone in search of blissfulness?

Richness

"Richness is not an accommodation to possess all you see and feel. It is a natural process to experience the thing in its fullest form".

You believe that people are associated with different attributes of life, to make themselves very popular through their status, which can be achieved with the power of money. Right, we all have been chasing this money since generation to generation, believing that we have to be competitively rich enough to impress other people in this world. Then, what are you living on this earth for? It is only to show and get appreciation from the surrounding people and that is what you regard as your greatest achievement in life.

But dear humans do understand that it's not money, status, fame or things as you assume. It is the abundance & prosperity which exists in different types of physical and nonphysical form. So, you can see and feel the richness that you experience here.

Only an individual can tell what richness means to them. Since richness in each person's life takes a different shape of experience. What form can richness be? It can be a materialistic form, human scene or any experience that makes us feel rich and give happiness in life.

Yes, we have to understand that richness is not only cash, wealth, luxury etc., but the experience that gives you wonderfulness in a situation, where there cannot exist any other expression than **"Richness"**.

Richness is always a complete, very higher mode of life; when you feel it, you will have the whole some. Yes, it should be that way. As you become more aware of your life, you will start to travel every part of richness and life will become miraculously unbelievable.

So, learn to experience the richness of life consciously, being aware of what is happening at every moment of your life. Do not generalise everything, life is happening in its own consciousness. Actually, it is not happening without consciousness. You and this universe are partners, where YOU display

Human consciousness + Universe consciousness = Your Life

As you spread your life around this beautiful world, do understand that it has its own richness, which is meant and exists for your experience. There is no rule in which you have to experience this richness. It depends upon how much of you, are in that present moment and accepting the flow of life. As you go through the flow of life, richness in every form keeps flowing in your life abundantly.

Just be open enough to receive all the richness that is available in this universe. Don't put any limitations to your thoughts and life. Bring all the wonders in life by understanding that everything is always for you to experience and understand that life is full of possibilities where the real essence of richness is hidden within.

Greater spiritual gurus & awakened people always lived a rich life by detaching themselves from any type of experience they have already undergone. As you become more generous with your life experience and being satisfied with what you already possess, makes your life unexplainably rich. So, hereafter do not look for richness in life, in the form of materialistic or physical form.

As you flow with life, richness always flows along with you, without any identification of reality that is happening to you all the time.

"You're born in richness, living in richness and always surrounded by richness. Only you have to accept and allow this richness to flow inside you. As you go with this process, even your external life will reflect its own richness in a different form which only you can understand".

Question yourself

1. How do you define richness in your life?
2. In what way will you celebrate your richness?

Believing

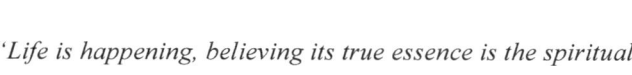

"Life is happening, believing its true essence is the spiritual. Being in connection always takes to the higher dimension where you are really blessed".

As you pursue the life you wish for, you tend to behave in a particular way, believing that you are meant to live a life of joy and happiness. It is really correct but do you know what you actually believe? Is it right that whatever you are following in life, is doing wonders for you? We do not know the proper answer since we believe that what ancestors and forefathers did in life, we are also meant to sustain and live the same life. We are not allowed to leave the society that we have been born in and brought up, believing that this is how we are destined to live.

Actually, we can live life as we wish but confined to a particular society of circumstances, we follow only the path that family or society has lived so far. Do we analyse and realise, whether we are doing everything in a correct way or going back on things that do not have any meaning blindfoldedly? In this case, only belief system exists but no reason of what actually we are doing here.

We are trained to believe in our system, society, education and the generation we are living in, but not letting us to analyse our life. To be specific, are we really living the life we want to live actually, not at all? It could be more effective if we just live more openly. Let us move forward to understand the existence of life on this earth. This existence, earth, nature, technology etc. - what do these things got to do with me? Why live on this earth? Don't I have any other planet to live? Do we have a choice to choose our existence? Such questions keep on arising, as we go deep into our life. When we take a break from life and look deep into the nature of our life, we really understand and believe the reality that we are not actually a sum of all these things. Since no one has the idea, why this existence is really happening? Do I have to cross examine everything in life? Why do we assume that we do not have the right to know about the life we are living?

As our understanding of life takes a different direction, all the good energy spirits and guides come into action to help us understand life. Where did all these good guides, spirits come from? They actually don't come from anywhere they have been within our existence already. But when we become more conscious and aware of our life, we get connected to higher energy. Here believing this existence of greater energy turns your life into a great bliss. Believe that there is greater attainment in your life, which knows the way you have to lead your life.

Consciousness and awareness are two rules of life to make your life more desirable and a place to live a great life. Only your belief in your greater energy will take you to the path of attainment of wisdom. No human can escape from this life. No escapism, you have to go through ups and downs. When your connection with God becomes stronger your life takes a shift to the other dimension, where only the person with consciousness and realisation can travel.

Believing the life that you are meant to live will make your life so magical, that unexpected things start happening and you will finally realise, the spiritual kingdom you are actually living in. Put further your reality of belief into a higher dimension of life, where a new door of life existence is waiting for you after death. But the path to death has to undergo all the pain and suffering to dissolve your karmic records. As you successfully get apart from all attachments, you will become enlightened through several journeys of life.

It is a great journey where you are meant to live in such a way, believing and understanding that some unseen power is waiting to connect to you and has opened divine hands to take you inside its enlightenment.

Question yourself

1. What is that belief system which changed your life?

Part 2

Depth Of Knowledge To Live (To Know)

Being Supernatural

Every human is a star who has been born on this earth. In this world everything is already aligned for you as per the birth of your soul. No human being is less than anything, they do not come to this earth to compare themselves with each other or fight for their survival.

Each and every human is allowed on this earth, to help each other in order to survive in this universe. As you grow without any interpretation of life's hustle, you become more conscious of your life. Generally, life on earth is full of super beings that come to live the life of joy and peace.

Most human beings have lost their consciousness by getting stuck with their personal problems. They have forgotten their purpose of life with the necessity to live the life of survival. Humans have been to this earth to clean up their past karma, but very few humans have this understanding.

There has been a great pressure for each human to just survive on this planet because it is full of unwanted misery and problems, where every human is submerged unconsciously and do not understand how to get out of it.

Many think that whatever they live and see is a natural thing happening to them. So, they compete with each other to prove their life, status, money, fame and many more things, thinking that the life they are living is real and the rest of do not understand -

"Why are we born and living?"

"Why are we all suffering with problems?"

Humans generally consider themselves as normal people who carry feelings, emotions and thoughts and live life as it takes them. But a large number of humans think that life they live cannot be changed and they are born to suffer. As well as, they do not realise that every problem that comes to their life is created by themselves and believe that they are not responsible for the suffering.

Every human has great power that is living within them. And the supernatural being is always trying to help them to live a prosperous life. But no humans realise that this supernatural being is really trying to help them come out of this karma (their actions). Understand the reality of how to stay connected with your being, which does a lot of miracles in your life.

Being supernatural doesn't mean flying, jumping or running. It is a being in your own state of joy, happiness and fruitfulness. The great being always tends to live in the happiest mode of life, living each moment in full of peace and bliss. You need not learn to operate to be supernatural, to live a wonderful life.

"You are already in the existence of life, where there is a real you who is living a great life within you".

You had never understood the inner being inside you. It is the real soul, who has chosen to live with you and also help you to have great enlightenment.

As you come to the state of blissfulness and peacefulness, life comes with an ease of understanding - How beautiful and grateful our life is? There has been a great divine timing, which invokes the light into you without any delay.

You have always been identified as a real being. But the real being is not you; it is the soul that has chosen to live within you. As there is a need for a lot of understanding to become a real supernatural, only awareness with consciousness will help you to become supernatural.

We all are actually born as supernatural beings, but our physical body makes us unable to understand the real ability to have a supernatural life. People, who are all born to some sort of unhappiness, pain, fear, etc., find it very difficult to realise their real super being.

You were born as a supernatural being. As you grow in this conditioned life, you lose your supernatural abilities and thus live a life full of unwanted problems, worries and fear.

A human will only realise their supernatural being only when time comes - karma should be dissolved.

The nature of being in joy, bliss, peace, happiness and full of love for others and self, creates a supernatural being. It is not a difficult task to do so, as said. We are living with a karmic version and we have totally forgotten that we all are supernatural. There is no great exercise to achieve. It is understanding the life's reality with awareness that each individual possesses all the power within themselves.

The supernatural being when accelerated, become the real god of their own life. And they become enlightened sources, where they understand what life process has stored for them.

Question yourself

1. Have you ever felt that you are a supernatural being?
2. What triggers your supernatural behaviour?

The Interlink

In human life everything is connected to one another. We need to mainly understand that each life on this earth is always linked to their soul particle. Similarly, every mind and thought is linked to each other where in return, they are linked to the body and soul.

Every human has many energy links from where it flows from one source to another through their thoughts, energy, vibration and frequency. We have to clearly understand that all the thoughts humans generate are linked to energy in a particular way, which creates a particular vibration and gets linked to another higher vibration source.

There is a lot of interlink generated between each human soul that creates their desired life. Every human assumes that they are the only individuals, who are surviving this life on earth. But knowingly and unknowingly they are interlinked with one another.

So many thoughts are generated in the human mind. Each thought is linked to a particular energy which in turn repeatedly manifests into a situation, person or a material. Thoughts are always generated in one's own mind. But who is generating a thought in mind? It is surely the source particle called **GOD**.

The source particle or God particle is bringing forth different thoughts into a mind, depending upon the karmic records being held. As one's karma, people generate good and bad thoughts that decide the future life unconsciously. Our thoughts do not allow us to live the life you want to live.

Our life goes through ups and downs in life, it is all because of our mind that manipulates and believes these thoughts and energies to be real and manifest accordingly.

The mind is not stable for most human beings because there is always a charter in their mind. A particular thought never lets a person be peaceful. Humans have to learn to discipline their thoughts, control their mind, only then a human life would be blissful.

Mind has greater responsibility to keep one's personal life relaxed or put in trouble. You are not bothered by thoughts that are flowing into your mind because you are living an unaware and an unconscious life.

This unconsciousness and unawareness of thoughts convert to a conscious one, only when your karma is cleared up. As your karma clears slowly, you come to the consciousness of life and take control of your mind and generate healthy thoughts, which in return make your body and soul happy.

As your soul is happy, you start to generate a lot of good manifestations and life becomes blissful and happy. There is a great interlink chain between thought, mind, energy, body, vibration and their soul. They are some-how interlinked with each other. Where one wrong thought affects everything in life but we humans very rarely realise these effects, as we are unaware.

We have to realise that at least our thoughts are only creating our day-to-day life, vibrating in a particular frequency, which slowly one after the other creates future life. Hence it is necessary for every human to understand the type of thoughts, we generate and live with.

Question yourself

1. What is that one thing interlinked in your life?
2. When have you felt that you are interlinked with other beings on this earth?

Universal Dimensions

There is a large existence of different dimensions in this universal world. It is in every form of different dimension, where even you are in a particular dimension living on this earth. As we perceive, there may exist universes unknown to us, beyond the scope of our research. We humans are trying to reach every dimension of our life through science with the help of researches.

Greater knowledge is to be acquired, not only through research but also you need to experience it. As you keep on experiencing new things in the dimensions you live, you are bound to have a lot of new shifts in your life. There exist many dimensions in different variations that human minds have realised. It is our responsibility to understand :

Why are we living this life?

What is happening to us, living in a particular dimension?

Greater knowledge is like wisdom that always flows from different dimensions to make us realise,

"Why are we living on this planet and what work do we have to perform?"

Many more things are answered to all the questions, we have in our mind. Since the human mind thinks in a lot of ways, that we do not understand, "What has this wisdom got to do with itself?"

You have to understand that this human being is a very great being and highly, spiritually connected to itself. But many do not understand that they are the living spiritual souls residing in the body of human beings. The Soul always tries to come out and wants to help us throughout our life journey. As our karma plays a very important role, it never allows a human to realise, "What is the purpose for living on this earth, and which dimension do we still exist in?"

There are different dimensions that exist in these multiple universe. Many of the extremely wise people have realised that there are many dimensions which are in an unimaginable state.

In a very higher dimension, there exists the highest source or God particle which transcends a lot of information into the human brain in the form of thoughts. As we understand and realise that a real being, a being spiritually aware, only joins the real God. More and more conscious awareness is needed to understand the dimension, we are living in now.

Dimensions in these universal places go in greater form as we grow spiritually while changing our life, as being in joy, happiness, peace and harmony. When you live your life so intently you reach the higher dimension with the help of the Soul you are living with. Each dimension can be reached only through the thoughts you carry and it will be executed by connecting to our emotions. Since emotions play a very great role in experiencing the dimensions we live in, emotions like fear, anger, guilt, worry, sadness, etc., don't let us shift to the higher dimension. As we become spiritually low, our emotions stop us from reaching our soul particle.

Controlling our emotions in a proper way will take us to higher dimensions, where you will come to an understanding that whatever life you are living is actually in an illusion stage. Attaining enlightenment is through the higher dimensional energies which connect to you where you become so pure and conscious.

Apart from human knowledge and wisdom, there also exist more dimensions, where it is believed that, even there is existence of life in different forms, with larger consciousness, which is trying to connect the Highest Source Energy from where they came.

The highest dimensional energies are a great form of light energy, from where everything originates to materialistic and non-materialistic life, creating illusion in human life and other beings in this universal source.

We have to learn to come across the dimensions in order to reach the light energy. But bad karma always keeps us in an unconscious state, not letting us come to the awareness about the illusion of life which exists in different dimensions. Only God's grace or blessings will help you to come out of the unconscious life of drama, which we are not really meant to live in.

The experience of different universal dimensions is compulsory for every human being which they will come across after many rebirths as per the karma they carry. Finally, they reach the source that is the God particle always existing in the form of light energy.

The Universal Dimension Choice

In our regard we all tend to live in the dimension of space and time. Each and every individual living in this universe is surviving on different levels of dimensions. No human has realised, where they are living and what they are living for? It is greatly important for every human to understand their choice of living on this planet. Different types of dimensions are already present in this universe, which are meant to give greater wisdom of understanding.

Not every human lives in the same dimension. Each and every human, according to their wisdom of consciousness, make them live in several dimensions.

One who attains enlightenment tends to live in higher dimensions, which cannot be seen or felt while being with that person. Normal people need to have greater realisation of what is going on within them. And we also need a real analysis within ourselves to attain higher dimensions for enlightenment. The dimension choices are only available when a karmic account is really cleared out. We cannot decide whether to reach particular dimensions until and unless we have greater blessings from the Source Energy. **Practicing Self Love is the first step for Self-realisation**. It really takes us to another dimension of life. As we become a real, pure soul full of love, happiness, joy, bliss, harmony, compassion and many more good things which allow humanity to survive on this earth.

As your soul becomes pure you are enlightened with universal wisdom, which is full of consciousness and awareness. This gets you to another level of living where you get to understand that the life you are living is now an illusion.

Even though we have many choices to live in this dimension, going to another level of dimension only happens with lot of universal blessings, which when meant to happen, will happen and nobody can stop it. If you are destined to live in another dimension, it has to be always kept practicing and search all the means of ways to reach the higher dimensions through your real-life purpose.

Unconditional Love

"Be the person of Love which never conditions you, as well as you never taken the right to condition others".

When you love someone without any conditions or expectations, it transforms into Unconditional Love, which never expects anything from anyone. It does not respond to the reaction of one person shown to another.

Many of them think that Unconditional Love is to love more than the opposite person but it does not work in this way. It is not a kind of love that reflects on your behaviour, attitude or type of love you show on others.

Unconditional Love is divine love where there may be or may not be any reflection for the love you have for the person. The love is so pure; it is a compassionate love, free from expectations.

We have to always understand that **God's Love - Source Love is Unconditional Love.** God is not biased with the love it gives us. It does not see any discrimination like rich, poor, cast, creed, religion, status, good or bad. God Love is our Higher Source Love, showered on us even though we do not respect it. Our inner soul always has unconditional love which is the ultimate character of a soul. A soul always tells us to be nice, compassionate to others. But we do not realise all these things because of the unawareness in life we are living.

More people are locked into the emotions of the thoughts which are making their life miserable. A normal human being always has a habit to receive something for the given things. Similarly, if we are giving or showing love to somebody, we expect someone to be more loyal to us and give more love than we have given to them. Moving one step ahead we think that they have to be our slave, listening and doing to whatever we tell them to do. Since this types of love exists between different relationships and very soon this type of relationship breakups or there is no satisfaction in their future life.

An Unconditional Love is to let others live the happiest life in the way they want to live, irrespective of what they are.

Unconditional Love always looks odd or people consider the person as a fool who possesses the nature of Unconditional Love. Because a human society thinks everything in this world is given and taken. Similarly, it is also for the love you have for the person, you should get benefitted from the love you carry within yourself for others.

Unconditional Love does not label anything or anyone. It gives full freedom for a person to live their life the way they want to live and enjoy the freedom of happiness. It is the result of Unconditional Love of a person.

You are a God of yourself and you should possess the nature of Unconditional Love, as energy that circulates within the body making you feel blissful all the time. Love is God's nature, so let every human at least learn to understand that love without condition would bear large fruits of joy, happiness and freedom for yourself and others.

Teach and learn to love people around you unconditionally, give all the freedom they want to live. Watch how beautifully people live their life on their own, it is the real Unconditional Love, you can give to others.

Most relationships in different forms always suffer without the non-availability of Unconditional Love. Many people have decided that loving someone is a rule or responsibility that we have to carry and we have to take control of other people's lives too.

Always be the god of love, full of freedom, peace, joy and happiness where it makes you truly happy without any condition. You have come to the earth to live a happy and prosperous life bonded with Unconditional Love. Similarly, others also have the same purpose to live on this earth. You have to understand that every human born on this earth is to be surrounded with a lot of Unconditional Love, which allows them to live the life they want to live.

You will become God of your own for all the Unconditional Love you give others and to yourself. You are a divine being bestowed with lots of love, which is the only solution for every problem in life.

Unconditional Love is the only solution in your life for every problem you undergo and helps to clear all your karmas.

Question Yourself

"Understand you are the question and you are the answer. Don't search it anywhere."

Are we living the life we want to live? How great is life? Did I know any answers for this? Do we have time to analyse ourselves? Like this, there arise a lot of questions within us. But we are not sure whether we are getting the appropriate answer or at times we lie to ourselves to escape the reality of life.

We never ever try to analyse ourselves very deeply. Because we assume that these things of questioning ourselves are unwanted things and how is that going to make a big difference in our lives. We think that nobody has given such an explanation, why do we need to question ourselves and what is the real use of doing that. As told by ancestors, we are said to follow their footsteps of life, to carry our life to the next level. But are we really aware of what we are doing as they did? There is nothing to blame them. Because they preached, what their elders had told them. Very few people analysed that - Are we living a true and correct life? Are we in oneness with our inner self?

As the days are going forward, we are all held up in the artificial world, where we have everything to satisfy ourselves easily but humans never find peace in anything. This is how humans are living in their present moment.

As we start moving away from the reality of life, we start losing ourselves in this illusion world and we become ready to pick our guilt, stress, depression and all sorts of things that make life more difficult.

Humans born on this earth are programmed in such a way that they are born to suffer on this earth and further they have to take life only through difficulties. Actually, life is very easy if we really understand our life system.

In so many ways, our higher self is trying to awaken us from the life drama and make us enter the life of consciousness. Since we are not properly told or understood, that our life we live is full consciousness. Because many people feel astonished by these words CONSCIOUSNESS, AWARENESS, HIGHER SELF, etc. Humans misunderstand the people who are speaking about the reality, thinking that they are some different species that have arrived from another universe. The normal people engaged in unawareness believe the illusion they are caged in, believing that's the life they are meant to live.

But how many great people, gurus and great rituals are always trying to awaken the inner reality of a soul, which is waiting to come out and make us realise "What type of life we have to live? What is the purpose of life we are living?"

So even though there is no awareness, you better question yourself, each and everywhere while you live on this earth, so that you will know what you have been doing on this planet. Humans are here to follow certain rituals like get educated, have a job, get married, reproduce another set of unaware humans, get old and die. This is not the game we need to play here. The purpose here is to help each other and serve the people around us. We are born to live a happy and prosperous life here. We humans are really meant to get connected with our inner self. It is meant to be our SOUL purpose, serve our soul's requirement and get enlightened so that you can reach the higher self, from where you came.

Any questions you ask yourself will always make you grow. No question or self-questions never put you down but make you understand, what really you are? Your inner self is waiting to explain the answer for all the questions that you need to ask.

Do you want to resolve your life problem? Want to be in peace and understand the purpose of life? Then be in connection with your inner self, which is ready to answer all the questions you have had about your life.

Better stop questioning the outside life, turn your focus internally, and ask :

"Why is the world not supporting me?

Why are people around me not good?

What do I have to do to succeed in this life?"

We have so many questions similar to this from birth to death but the best advice is, don't question your external world. Instead turn towards yourself and ask your inner self.

"What is waiting for me to serve the purpose of life on this earth?"

Your questions will be answered in such a way where there will be a great shift experience. As you become conscious, our life starts answering you for everything, for the questions you are asking within yourself.

Reincarnation

The word Reincarnation is a fantasy word, which makes us feel that it is holding something very big.

Rebirth of nature, humans, species, animals and everything in this universe is happening again and again unknowingly. No human has seen above a certain amount of knowledge, to understand the process of incarnation. It is a very big theory, working in a particular formula in a precise way at a divine timing.

Reincarnation is a very great and huge subject behind the human imagination. You all living beings deserve to know your purpose of birth and death. Everything is happening again and again, starting from birth to death. There has been a great evolution of living energies into different forms in a different way. You have been chosen by the greater universal Source Energy, that where you have to be and what you have to be. It is a very strange unknown process of life from a single cell to multidimensional cell, where some are in physical form and some in the unidentified form.

We humans still don't understand the full concept of Reincarnation and it is not a limited subject to just finish just like that. Rebirth/Reincarnation whatever the words we use there is always a deep meaning engraved inside it.

Because no humans have known -

Where has it started? Why did it start? When will it stop?

"Reincarnation is a great consciousness concept. Only it (GOD) knows - What energy incarnates into what type of energy bodies. Since all the things in reality and unseen things in non-reality are only decided by the Highest Source Energy which still no one has defined it".

We people are making such efforts and researches to know what is happening, within us and around us. But still our knowledge and wisdom combined have not gone so further to understand the process of the **HIGHER BEING.**

Generally, we humans have realised through scientific and spiritual studies that every living and non-living thing on this earth has to play the game of death and birth again and again according to karmas, we have performed during the living period on this earth.

So, as we are Reincarnating into different forms from plants to animals, humans to animals or in form of any physical reality to nonphysical reality everything is decided only by the actions of our karma in that particular birth.

This rebirth purpose does not make us remember anything about the previous birth and the type of life we have lived because if we remember a past birth, we would not be able to live this life peacefully.

If we are lucky with karma, we get to be born as humans because it is the best form of life where only the humans have the choice to get **SOUL ENLIGHTENMENT** or **SPIRITUAL AWAKENING**. Born as humans is the rarest thing that can happen to you, since human beings only have a chance to become the light energy and reach your **Highest Source Energy.**

Any other form of rebirth apart from human beings is a very difficult process in gaining spiritual awakening and attaining enlightenment.

So, every human has to understand and realise how lucky we are to have been born on this earth as humans. It has such a great power to be a human, where you have all deliberate chances to get yourself enlightened. But very few gain the real knowledge of reincarnation and most of them do not have any realisation of these types of unaware realistic things. They do not get to know that birth and death of humans several times is a repeated game which we humans never understand.

In reincarnation your karma plays a very important role and it is the only decision-making part that decides the type of rebirth we have to take as soon as we die. Many things come and go in this universe repeatedly because everything is a game of death and birth in different forms, not knowing where to start and where to finish.

We need a great blessing of God to come out of this birth and death game. Where only our Highest Source Energy decides whether a death is a meaningful end or rebirth has a purpose again to perform an action.

"Better play a safe game when you have been born on this earth as living beings, otherwise you will be caught in the loop of death and birth cycles".

Every human tries to pray and get blessings of God as early as possible because humans have no time to nullify their karmic debts. As soon as possible mankind has to realise their purpose of life and attain enlightenment in order to reach the Higher Source of Energy, from where you came.

Reincarnation is only the process of making your human energy into a divine form by resolving your karmas.

Reincarnation is the filtering process of divine energies, where the best redefined pure energies become the part of HIGHER CONSCIOUSNESS ENERGY.

Undeveloped Thoughts

"Before you water any thoughts in your mind, be in an aware stage of consciousness that what you reaped was already sowed only by you".

Great, great engineering works in our life are done only through thoughts we have processed. Here engineering does not go by profession. It is actually the buildup or creation of any materialistic life through proper processing of thoughts.

Every thought we carry always results in its own way by the depth of the emotions we had put on the particular thought. All thoughts are necessarily getting manifested knowingly and unknowingly. We humans generally are not that conscious and aware whether our thoughts have really created a scene, a material or any other scenario because humans' life is full of thoughts and its process.

We humans live a very casual life of not understanding how much of our life has been manipulated with the thoughts we had. There is nothing to blame but unawareness of life that we are living, is leading to all sets of circumstances, which can sometimes be good or bad. The thoughts that came to your mind were always unexpected. A human not being cautious gives life to a thought not understanding whether the thought is needed or not. We humans need to know what type of thoughts need to be pushed away from our life.

Okay! Where do these thoughts come from? Who knows? Only God knows! Yes, it is right, only the Highest Source Energy - God is emitting all the thoughts in our mind and mind plays the chords of thoughts, depending on what type of situation we are currently living in.

When we are emotionally low, our thoughts become weak, in a way, a series or a bunch of thoughts keep flowing nonstop and they never stop, until we strongly try to quit those unwanted thoughts. People always think about things that make them emotionally sad or past thoughts which give a good feeling for what has already happened.

We humans normally never try to inspect our thoughts even though we are having thousands of yielded thoughts in our mind. We can take control over it by being more severely conscious and aware of what is really happening within us.

The thought which is not given any importance or left free seems not to develop further to create any unwanted situation. We humans get to discipline emotions so that when any thought appears, the undeveloped thoughts whether good or bad never disturb your life. It will tend to keep your life very blissful when unwanted thoughts are not manifested. These undeveloped thoughts are like weeds in a rice field which have nothing to do and can be safely pulled off when not really required.

Better you learn and get educated on how to handle the thoughts. Be more aware of which thoughts need to be processed. If a thought is processed it should give a good result or value for your life process. Here I would mention that not every thought can be taken care of but as much as possible try to be very disciplined and conscious in handling your thoughts.

Always understand that your thoughts are creating your life. Your thoughts are the seed, which is sowed in your mind soil to yield a healthy plant. Be always sure what type of seed is being sowed in your mind daily.

The Indefinite Layers

We do not have a lot of understanding about our life journey. And very rarely we give importance to our life that we are struggling to live. What is the necessity to live life like this, where we do not sustain in the position of life until our blessings stay with us?

We as humans and different creatures on this earth have their own survival level which cannot be described very precisely. Everything is unknown at a level of our understanding. Guru's, our divine spiritual teachers who have led their life to reach a great place of divine energy, have revealed so many things that even human imagination does not have any idea. We humans are not what we see at the present moment. Many or most have no realisation of what is really going around them as well as what is happening within them.

We humans have never bothered so much to know about the reality of this life because everybody, even many people in the old generations are not even aware of the essence of the life, we have come to live on this earth.

But the actual reality is that we are living in different layers of life where we think that everything is happening at the level of earth's dimension. Every happening has its own layers (to understand assume as levels). Every human or any individual is not living in the same plain.

According to their karmic debts they are performing the actions at their designated layers. Everything for us seems like the same layer but we are not aware about the indefinite number of layers that are lying between each human life.

Can we see the indefinite layers that are differentiating our lives at different unassumed levels? These layers of life on which we are living cannot be seen or counted but it can be felt when you become more conscious of the life process.

Considering in depth of your body, there are so many layers, not only that even your aura is full of different layers. In nature, the sky itself has many different layers but science tells that there are definite layers. As we travel to the space and solar system, can we tell how many layers of plains exist and might be there is an existence of life in indefinite layers in different forms?

Who on this earth has assumed the indefinite layers of earth? No living thing has found the unseen layers which are not in human consciousness.

We don't know in which dimension, in which layer, in which universe we are existing in order to resolve our karmic debt that has made us take the human shape so that we can dissolve all the karmas which have been travelling along with us very definitely.

There is no escapism for any creature born on this planet. Each and every one cannot run away from their own karma because we all have come here to perform that particular action so that our karmic debts will get dissolved and with the **"GOD - THE HIGHEST**

SOURCE ENERGY BLESSINGS." You will be transformed as light energy by attaining the process of enlightenment.

Do always understand the process and always remember an unknown blessing is always waiting for you to shower all the goodness on you.

Believe the inner source - the connector of the highest source - the provider of salvation from birth to death.

Electrify Yourself

"You are the SOUL. You are the ENERGY - electrified to lighten your life to bombard the universe with the power you hold and get dissolved in the Higher Source – GOD".

Anyone or anything done in excitement gives the best result out. Yes! Absolutely. You know, how good it would feel while there is a best experience.

The power inside you is the real energy, which keeps on electrifying you at a greater level in unexpected ways. You should always know the power existing has all the ways to perform any type of action to boost your life towards better living. We humans have to understand that we are wonderful beings in different forms of character, believing this is the real thing. But actually, to say you are a morphed being of spirituality.

To have a great understanding of yourself, you need to move deep inside yourself or look inside you and ask - What am I doing here? Am I really doing all this stuff? Yes, you are the real spiritual being to be known with all the electrified sources that lie beneath you. You need to pull that energy source from within, to show your electrifying performance to the world. You need not act or behave in a different way. But get connected to the soul that is waiting to connect to you. This old soul knows more than anyone, what is the real thing you need to do in this lifetime. Catch hold of yourself very tightly and just sit quietly. Soul will show its power that you have never realised as well as not expected.

Great, great beings always electrified their soul energy to such a greater level that they slowly pushed up higher to show what a magnificent power they were.

You see so many people give an electrifying performance which is beyond their reach. Do you think humans mastered it? Not at all, it's their **"SOUL'S PERFORMANCE"**. It knows where to hike you with the connection you hold.

Be pure as much as possible because you do not know how good it will become when it comes out powerful from within. Pull it out with all your power, to do it you need to have a lot of consciousness and awareness. As well as how well you are connected to your being.

Once you have got connected to the soul power then something wonderful is about to happen without any hard work. It will perform everything on your behalf. Leave it or surrender to your soul, it will put you on the path of attainment of love and compassion, where your life will be so easy that you will never have anyone to compare or judge it.

Electrify each and every part of your life to enjoy this being on this earth. Boost the soul by your love, compassion & happiness, where it triggers your life energy in such a way that you become unique on your part. You will understand how powerful you have been all these years.

Life is always more important to you than any other thing because you have come to perform the action that you are meant to do here. But humans really struggle to sustain their happiness.

You no longer need all these materialistic things to be happy. Just wire yourself to the soul energy and switch it on with love and compassion. Here you glow so magnificently, so brightly that everything moves towards you by not even moving a single thing.

Get electrified in each and every moment of life you get to live. Let your performance bloom, making others envy you. Always understand humans, everything starts and ends with you but only you have to realise how to do it. The action and result are always within you. Be ready to perform what you have been meant to be doing. Do understand, you always come here to serve - nothing else than that.

Question yourself

1. Which moment you where electrified to understand your soul?

Layers Of Life

Do we know where we stand in this life? Where are we living this life? No proper answers. Since most of us are still living in unawareness, not understanding why we are living here.

The great things that are happening on this earth are very much to be appreciated other than looking towards its creativity. Every life on the earth is a creation of God which is actually to be appreciated. Every part and area of life has something meant for us which we have not tried to understand at all. Why is the understanding of life not coming to us easily? It is because we all are living life in different layers of feelings and emotions.

What do the layers of life got to do with us? Everything in human life is led by emotions of each and every thought we have created. We have to realise that thoughts run our life. Every thought flows in different layers. It can be layers of your guilt, pain, loss, failure etc. We not only have layers that create a life to undergo pain and suffering, but we humans also carry different layers of happiness, love, goodness and joy.

Our life is a combination of layers that brings goodness and sadness. The layers we trigger in our life come into our being. The more you trigger the layers of same feelings and emotions are created and further it creates a future and encompassing of the emotions and feelings.

As we realise there are always repeated layers of same feelings or thoughts, we need to know what is really needed in our life. When humans become very conscious and aware of their own being, they understand what layers of emotions and feelings, they have constructed in their life and which are manipulated into a real form.

Most of us are entangled in different layers without realising that these layers are creating our life's reality. And we humans find it okay to live in this type of a situation where our life gets bored and irritated. Even though we are ready for it and still suffer in the hold of different layers. Our soul is still in love and compassion with us and is waiting to help us all the time. The inner self of each and every one always knows how to bring out of suffering and pain. It is your real guru which sheds light onto the path you have to reach.

You become so aware that your soul talk is always heard by you. You just follow every instruction or intuition, without doubt or a second thought and do it. In this universe more than anything else your inner self is the only belief which is working inside you, taking you to the path of enlightenment.

Believe in yourself. Yourself is your inner being, the God always loves, guides and knows better than anything else what you actually need for this life purpose.

Traditional Career

"Always realise that no human is born to suffer but to live a life of purpose, of serving and helping people around you - Your Traditional career"

The work that we always perform has some action to benefit us. It can be a simple performance or heavy but it is an important work we have performed. Then what type of work do we all do? Everyone has their work from different categories, methods, ideas to perform in order to keep their life upgraded.

In this world, everything present is built upon the hard work of each and every human, which has made human life more cultured, comfortable and luxurious. But are we really feeling the comfort of living? I don't mean the riches you enjoy, where it makes you live as you desire to live without any resistance or difficulty in mind. We have got all that we wanted from the luxury and riches we hold. Everything has become easy for us and whatever we desire comes to us easily.

Okay, if so, then why aren't all rich and comfortable zoned people stressed and not realising what type of actual life they are living? Here I am not to blame anybody, I am just telling you that when everything in this world is easily available to you, there is still something missing in your life which you are still searching for.

Really! You do not understand what you have been doing for so many days in your life. You have just performed some actions that are giving you temporary happiness through materialistic things. You would have now realised even though you made your life comfort and luxurious, that card of happiness is not available for you.

Why all are undergoing so many difficulties and sufferings? What is the purpose of living on this earth, which does not give us what we want in life permanently? Yes, this is the voice that is gushing up into everybody's life. What do we have to do to be happy?

The only thing that can be said is to just go back to your traditional career. Does this raise a question mark in your head? Yes, truly to say we have all been lost in the chain of pain, suffering, fear and other big entanglements in this materialistic life. We all are running behind this unwanted life and have forgotten to work in our traditional career. Our Traditional career is not something to do or to follow. Actually, we have been doing all these things during the earlier days of our ancestors.

Our ancestors always lived with nature, they moved with the flow of nature and allowed nature to guide, protect and take care of them. They were always dependent on nature for everything in their life. This type of living always gave them peace of mind, good vibes and connection with the universal energies. This universal energy is in the form of nature which lets you live life in all its goodness, bliss and always bring the realisation to you that we humans are also an integral part of this nature.

Apart from nature, ancestors did always what actually humans needed and never affected the life of others. Because our ancestors' lives were full of things in abundance and they were self-sufficient since this universal mother nature had everything to provide them. In this way, our ancestors did what nature told them. They did the work that only made them happy. They always performed the action that made their soul happy.

Our great, great grandparents were really soul connected people. They were never as stressed out as we are now. They did the job that helped other human beings and the other types of living beings happy. They always lived in a loving community, easily forgiving people, finding happiness in all the little things they had in life and only took nature's fresh food, which always kept them healthy and fit for long years. They lived as nature always wanted them to live, always flowed along in the direction of nature and was always connected to the inner self, which was continuously guiding them.

These people had no distractions or disturbances in life. They were always living in the present moment, enjoying each and every moment they lived. Everyone worked with nature and energies. They always believed in the universal law and knew only it was the guiding map. At present also few of them consider our ancestors as God or divine and worship them. These very great old generations were the living gods. They knew how to manipulate energy and everything happened according to their wish.

But nowadays, we people have been caged in the name of luxury and comfort and have moved away from nature. We all are believing and will always be believing, that this material life would give us everything that is necessary for our life.

Dear people understand that everything you see around your existence, living and every non-living thing is only an illusion, that is running the life of every human for all who have good and bad karmas.

Only very few have escaped this illusion filled karmic life, following their traditional career by loving, helping and forgiving people around them. Many have tended to follow the path of great gurus, to escape this illusioned karmic life.

Every human has a purpose to live in a unique way and for that reason you have been on this earth till now. All humans are blessed with their life's purpose job, which comes into being, when you follow your traditional career.

As part of life, we always keep on travelling to make ourselves motivated, to survive on this earth, but how far this has helped us to find ourselves? A question may arise, why should I find myself? I am already in this existence on earth. Yes, right all are living on this earth as a physical identity, believing to be real. But this is not the concept of existence in this beautiful world. We have come to this planet to perform a particular action that is meant for us. An action is nothing but to serve our life's purpose, it is mainly to serve people around us and uplift their life.

Then what is the need to have a traditional career? First understand that a traditional career is the primary basis of a survival living, where this career has different jobs to play, where you let yourself heal and help others to heal.

In different ways people can be helped to heal by teaching forgiveness, coming out of fear, avoiding to be guilty, freedom from being caged in the past, not to be worried about your future. These different emotions and thoughts held inside the human mind have caused suffering from generation to generation. But still we are following the same emotions and thoughts as a part of karma we have performed in our past life.

The wholesome job you have come to perform is to heal your life from guilt, fear, over thinking, worry, and many more so that you can dissolve your life's karma. For dissolving your karma that you have carried into this life is by becoming a traditional career holder. That is, you have to love, show compassion, forgive people, come out of fear, guilt and stop overthinking.

Above all learn to live your life in the present moment and be connected to yourself and all the things can be healed easily. Yes, at last it would be a very long story of healing. It might even take any number of lives to heal and dissolve your karma. So, your first and almost the best thing to do is to just get connected to your soul, which is the ideal part of life to get answers for your living.

Your soul is your divine - the only solution to heal and dissolve your karma - be always connected to your soul.

Shield Yourself

The lives of humans are getting complicated day by day. We are not realising and not even taking time to think. Why is our life becoming so difficult? Even though normal people enjoy all sorts of comforts, something is missing in their life. Where are we all going in our life? Is that how we are meant to live? Not at all! This is not the real life we are meant to live. There is something different waiting for us to do.

Unless you humans realise the reality that your own life is meant to be easy and simple, you have nothing to do with yourself. As the pain increases in human beings, the love for this life becomes difficult with hatred for everything and life seems impossible.

We do not find ourselves in our lives. Since we have made life more complicated than ever, we thought. Thinking that we are making our life more beautiful, actually we have made our life so miserable that we are not able to comprehend our own life. When we have made our lives so difficult, then what is the reason to live this life like this? Do understand you are not meant to live this life this way. You are a blessed being meant to live a life of blissfulness and peacefulness. But due to unconscious behaviour and thoughts our life flows through all miseries creating more and more problems and making life complicated than expected.

Are we going to live a life like this to the very end? Do we have any common sense to break the entanglement of life and make our life breathe? We are always reminded that in each and every moment, to be aware of our thoughts and live a conscious life. But we humans do not even get time to realise what type of life we are living and how will we shield our life. Have you any day taken a while to think how you will protect your life? Are we taking any measures to keep our life safe from unwanted things that are disturbing our beautiful life? Who is going to help us to keep our life safe? Nobody is going to save our life happiness. It is only you who has to do all the things. Don't feel heavy if I meant it for you, it is not the physical you, it is the real you - your **SOUL**. It knows better than everyone in this world. Hand over everything to it. Your **SOUL** knows and will tell you easily, how you can shield your life blissfully.

Your **SOUL** is the master of everything. It is an old **SOUL**, experienced a lot more than anyone expected. It is very much focused and has a designated role to play in your life. Just strive a little hard to get connected to this mass powerful energy (**SOUL**) which can bring miracles in your life and can lead you to the path of righteousness. It keeps you on track throughout your lifetime nonstoppingly, but you are not listening to the inner voice which is always speaking, because your external voice is much louder.

Our internal voice is creating a lot of ways to make us survive on this earth but you never get to do this. Just surrender yourself to your **SOUL**. That's all, your life is done and everything happens in a beautiful way. You will be cherished in a very beautiful and unexpected way, understanding how well your **SOUL** is guiding you. But this happens only when you are living a very mindful life.

SOULS are the best masters of your life. You need not a guru to take care of you. It can beautifully guide you when you are more conscious and aware of your thoughts. Just slow down, feel yourself and realise that it is a great existence trying to help you in every part of life.

You just need to gather all goodness in your life with your **SOUL'S** assistance. Just believe life is happening in its own way. It knows how important your life is to you. The **SOUL** is your guardian angel. Hold this guardian angel strongly, and your life will be set. Be ready to travel on to the path of **ENLIGHTENMENT** as early as possible.

Times Up

We are living life in urgency without even under-standing what we are actually doing, always rushing towards something or the other to fulfill our needs or someone else's needs. When would we stop and gasp for a moment to see. What are we doing now? We are still racing very hard to finish something in time. Have we actually made it possible? Always trying to fill the gaps where life has related emptiness, trying to replace one after the another, believing that there would be no time and space to do it.

Gradual changes always keep happening in their own way but when we assign a time to complete certain things everything becomes stressful. Moving randomly from one part to another part of life has become a normal routine for everyone. Have we come to earth to do all the unwanted things that do not match our feelings and emotions? Not at all but we are not actually worried about it. We just do as everybody does otherwise we would look different from the other people.

Okay, let's do whatever we want to do. But do we have enough time to live on this earth? Can anyone mention and give a guarantee for existence for a lifetime? We humans imagine and believe that there is a lot of time left over to live this life. Since our realisation of the reality of life has failed to make humans understand that there is very little time to pack your things and just leave this earth without any intimation. Have you come here only to be born, live and die? How long will you believe that this is your life structure? You have to understand that this illusion life you are living has nothing to do with you after death. Why do we need to understand life and know about our purpose of living on this earth? Is it necessary?

Nothing happens in this universe without any reason. Similarly, even your existence has a purpose to be delivered in a very particular time and space. We are the real light energies taking a different physical structure and performing a particular destined action as the karma beholds.

There is nothing for us to perform on this earth. You are just an entertainer of your life under someone's direction. A film story is already written and being directed on the earth plane according to the karmic records you hold.

A very large number of people are unaware of real-life existence because they are not conscious about the purpose of their birth. We have been engulfed into this illusion life believing that we have to live this life to sustain on this earth successfully. There is nothing like success and failure. It is all a man-made measure making humans forget and believe how powerless they are.

In reality no humans are powerless because every soul within an individual carries and defines the power in such a way which cannot be seen but felt. It is so powerful that even the electricity would fall in its highest frequency.

Do understand you are the real power of the universe that has come to the earth to achieve your purpose and live it in that form.

To summarise, you have come to this earth to dissolve all your karma's, unknowingly from many births and deaths you have gone through. This is not your first birth and death, you have already taken thousands of birth in order to dissolve your karma. But still believing in the illusion life attachment, you are not coming out of this dream life. Because you cannot see and feel them until your karma records have been nullified.

The realisation of who you are, will definitely bring changes in your life knowing that you do not have enough time to finish all the unwanted life issues and become the real **YOU**. Until you don't end the karma cycle you have to keep on taking birth into different forms of creatures and in different universes, in different dimensions. You will have to again suffer for what you are actually doing now. Just try to end everything in life slowly but quickly as soon as possible because you have no time. Complete all your karma under any spiritual guru's guidance and become enlightened, as much as possible. You have to know that your only achievement is to reach the Highest Source Energy and become one with that light energy that is waiting for you.

If you are still getting coiled into this illusion life of entanglement, when will you come to realise this? Whatever you are just living now is nothing; it is a useless memory of what you have been carrying in all your births and deaths.

Just fasten, before your times up for this lifespan and get out of this suffering. Do anything to just get rid of your real self out of the embodiment and become the oneness of creation.

Your creator is always waiting with open hands to grab all scattered power spilled throughout this multi-dimensional universe. Just put on a gear and fly straight at the earliest to reach your divine, who is waiting for you since a very long time.

Hurry up, **TIMES UP** to get enlightened - Become oneness with your Highest Source Light Energy.

Taking Help

"Life is to just surrender within yourself so that the reflection on external existence will greatly showcase how powerful you are representing on behalf of the soul".

We generally assume that we have a very balanced life. But we do not understand how much we struggle to keep our life balanced. The struggle you go through to make your life happy, is unexplainable. You are always making sure that you are happy but you do not experience any kind of happiness in your life.

You generate the happiness mode of life that only gives you what you have expected to have otherwise you think life is a disaster. Does it mean that life is so easy for you to feel the disaster? Not at all, life experiences are different situations of emotions creating a brand-new life at every stage even if you have expected it or not. Not realising how much suffering you are embedding in your life. You are again and again ready to make your life miserable and it is dejected enough to make it move to the next level.

Great experiences are received not only from the suffering you have undergone, but each moment of life is giving you great miracles, which are making you step into the next stage of a certain level where you never know, what is actually happening to you. You need not get frightened of life as new things keep on appearing in your life which is not understandable.

Every new experience creates a general idea of great confusion. Why is life happening? Why is it happening only to me? Every person undergoes different cultural shocks with reference to the dimensions of life they are living. Don't assume that people with wealth are all happy, it is not at all. Even they are trying different ways to be happy.

Do we need to struggle so much to keep ourselves in peace? I think it is not really necessary, if you really understand the meaning of life. When you get to know how life is happening for each one of them on this earth you will get to know about your purpose of existence.

So, who is going to help you on this earth? Do we need to find that person who would help? Yes, you need to find but not the person, **The God** inside you. You are the reflection of the soul, within you, showing how much you are connected. So, realise that consciousness is existing as **SOUL** within each one of us.

Your inner self is in the form of a greater energy source existing within, and is always helping you each and every time. Since we humans have collapsed in the external voices, we are not able to hear the communication of the inner soul, which is always guiding you.

Make yourself peaceful and stop over thinking only then you would be able to get connected to an inner soul and will be able to listen to the voices of your soul. You first might feel very difficult to get connected to your soul but as you practice, your connection with the soul becomes stronger. Don't feel ashamed to take help from your soul since your soul's purpose is only to assist you in every stage of life. And no better than your inner self knows, what is good and bad for you. It is always working for you, to take you to the path of justice as presided by the universe.

You have come to experience your karma, so that you can dissolve as early as possible. When you are strongly in connection with your inner self, your life becomes easy and you keep moving to the next dimension of life and get into the path of enlightenment.

Everything is easily available through the help of your inner self then why to worry about life. First, surrender yourself to your inner self, and it will take care of your whole life and put you in the awareness of life.

You are the life maker but just strive to take help of your soul to show, how purely you are existing in this earthly life.

Question yourself

1. Would you mind taking help rather than giving help to others?

Be Wise

We teach ourselves to endure in different aspects of life, to show our skill and talent. Humans have always tried to prove themselves to others and their external community, to show how well they are running this life. But actually, are you following the proper procedure? You have been scanning life all the time to show your society, that you have achieved something in every stage of life. Does this attainment of success at every stage of life give you peace & happiness?

You have still not stopped trying very hard until the end of your life so that you are able to prove yourself to others. You are not satisfied even though you have made the highest achievement in the world.

What gives an individual peace and happiness in their life? We all are always searching for something or the other in life. Are we getting answers for all the things we are searching for? Does the answer received give you satisfaction? No because you expected something but received something else in life. When the expectation of your life fails, it hurts you to a very great extent and creates a large irritation and tends to make you lose interest in life.

Why are we humans not finding life so interesting and what is making us so bored? A great question where the answer is very simple to realise **WHO YOU ARE?**

As the realisation of **WHO I AM** - generates great behavioural and emotional changes in your life. It would seem that something creepy is happening to you since there is no one around who is like you or as same as you. If you tend to speak to other people about what you are experiencing, they make fun of you and nail you to be mentally ill. Let it be so, but your awareness of yourself will increase and you will start becoming wiser. You will start to identify yourself beautifully as you are changing. As well as you become wise about what is the good and bad part of life that you have been doing all these years. You will become so determined to take only that action which is always right for you. You know something a huge power inside you is guiding you very closely.

As your wisdom grows you will have a great shift in dimension. You become so pure that all your karma starts falling apart and you feel very clean and empty. Being wise makes you live more easily and understandable for every day-to-day problem you are facing. It is not meant that there would not be any difficult situation in life. There would be a presence of everything in life but the way you realise your circumstance and handling it will be much clearer to you. You will stop stressing so much because you are aware that life is transforming something especially for you, where you are shifted to the next dimension.

Never assume that wise people are always self-realised people. It is not at all, self-realised people have great realisation on this illusion life but their awareness and consciousness are projected to the universe energy.

You become a genius energy when life is realised, so just keep doing what your inner guidance is telling you. You might not see the change immediately that something wise has happened to you. You will never ever again reflect on this unmatched world because you are blessed with divine power, holding all the universe consciousness within yourself very tactfully.

Be Alive

"Greater knowledge is known
Greater wisdom is unknown
But only wisdom finally edges the victory".

Are you sure to live this life very effectively? It is not meant to have status, richness, fame and a lot more that defines you. We are unaware of what defines us to the extreme level of life. There is always some search in life according to our existence but not sure what we are searching since we want everything to be better than others. As we keep on comparing our life stream, we do not feel very good since there is no satisfaction even when we are getting a better one. Our human mind always keeps on getting triggered by something or the other and not letting us rest in peace and we act according to our mind's reaction since we have become its slave.

We have generalised our life to live according to our minds' reaction not realising how bad our life's existence is turning up each and every second. As life flows usually without any clarity, you get to indulge in difficulties and suffering thus making your life more and more miserable. Each new moment is trying to give a new life but humans never understand the depth of life since we think a new life has to start after something great has happened.

We perceive each stage of life as it were a new beginning. It is not that way, every moment is trying to teach you something new that have not been present in the previous moment but lack of focus does not let us find any differences in our life situations.

Clear your mind in such a way that everything in life becomes something more than usual. You need to be more alive at each and every moment of life to understand your life journey. As you become more alive in your presence, you get to understand what that moment is presenting to you. So, when life is giving you some excellent opportunities both in times of suffering and happiness, you should be able to understand how the situations need to be handled by you.

Every situation is teaching you some or the other knowledge of realisation. Why is this happening to me and what are these circumstances trying to educate me? When you become keener to understand your life, you start to become more alive and your life takes another shift. Whereas this dimension of life is explaining to you what is the purpose for you being here.

As your awareness increases, life brings all sorts of situations to make you get practice on how to handle circumstances even if you are happy or sad. You will very soon learn to handle and accept your karma. You become more fearless as you believe that you are moving to the highest stage of wisdom which is set to attain enlightenment. As life becomes more understandable your soul connection becomes more beautiful, where it will guide and protect you as much as possible it is required for that situation.

Behavioural changes are sure to happen since you have realised the reality of life and you will start moving to the stage of silence by decreasing the arguments and over-thinking attitude. A feeling of peace at very regular intervals starts to be experienced by you and will give you more wisdom for your inner realisation. The changes in your mind, body and thoughts uplift you to a very greater height that no one can see. Only you will feel the peace and easiness in life. In every situation of life, you will become more active in order to live a very beautiful life that is meant for you.

So be rigid in keeping yourself (SOUL) and your mind peaceful than any other thing, which will bring more goodness to you.

You are chosen and blessed, gifted with a precious wisdom which cannot be bought with any amount of money. Enjoy this rejuvenated life, make everything easy for you and always be available for everyone with your love and compassion.

The Sword

Every word you speak reflects your behaviour, attitude and thoughts. Words are the tools of our communication. It slowly blends our life reality knowingly and unknowingly. There is a great reality that is hidden from us where these words bring out the life's situation without our knowledge. You have been always told to **"Think before you speak"** but we humans don't think before and don't think even after we speak because all the words flow easily from our mouth, when we want to speak. Our mind always tries to manipulate us by triggering our feelings and making us speak as we like but not realising that these words are not going to give any satisfaction for what we have spoken.

Great knowledge comes to you as you silence yourself by not speaking. Since every spoken word is very important as it produces particular frequency and bring that world's reality into physical form. Be careful while you communicate, put a lot of concern into your mind and ponder on what type of word is flowing into your mouth.

Every word you speak creates a specific frequency and energy, creating an entanglement in the universe. Each and every word is very powerful as it designates what your character and behaviour is. You always think certain bad words come out when you are triggered or sometimes we have a habit to speak rubbish. Let it be any type of words, everything produces a sound that very greatly influences the universe which cannot be seen.

Most of the words we speak sometimes hurt people or are soothing and encouraging. But most of the time the sound produced from our mouth hurts people not realising how much the person opposite to you is hurt **"Every word is a sword"**. So better be very conscious and careful while you are attempting to sound.

You might be thinking about what a word can do. A word or sound being energy always keeps creating different types of vibrations, which installs new karma for the words you have spoken. Anything would not reflect very immediately, sometimes it takes time. Words make miracles in our life thus we use a lot of good vibrating words to pray. Believing it reaches God's ears. Actually, everything in this world is an existence both of physical and non-physical form but we don't realise how all these things take shape.

Every single word is like a sword, use it very carefully wherever and whenever it is needed. You have to be wise enough to handle the words that come out of your mouth. Be very conscious of what you start to speak and understand what type of situation you are in. Don't try to win the conversation or situation by harnessing the words. You don't have to win situations all the time by speaking. Silence creates victory in most of the situations. You never have to be very loud to speak. Speak in the mode of audibility of people around. Because each word and sound produced by us along with non-physical things, always keep vibrating in the universe, creating another reality without our knowledge.

It is really a practice to always keep some check on the words you have spoken, because even our great gurus are very careful with words and sounds. They very cleverly used it to create mantras, magic, mysticism in their personal life. Sound produced and mingled with universe energy in a different form of reality apart from our knowledge comes into being.

So don't only use words just to express yourself but be disciplined. Even the plant and non-living things can carry the energy of the frequency which even influences them. As you become more conscious of your life, you will start seeing and experiencing miracles and mysticism in your life. Then you will soon realise how important it is to be careful with the words.

As you produce words or sounds, be in full awareness to create the world you want. Everything is energy and everything has energy. Be mindful and careful to handle your life. Don't let anyone manipulate your life with their thoughts and ideas, even some words keep manipulating our life situation.

Don't fall prey to some other people's decisions and ideas. You are a unique gem to be borne on the crown of heaven.

Trust Yourself

Be sure that you always trust yourself more than any other thing in life. You are the first important person in your life. No one is more important than you. You have to strongly catch hold of yourself, so much that nothing can tear you apart. Actually, saying even if you don't catch hold strongly no one has the power to make you separate from your real self. You are not identified for what you are like name, status, family, career, etc. You are a separate identity, surviving within a physical body and bringing all the experiences to navigate through this life.

Life has all its teachings through sufferings and experiences. The human who accepts it totally gets through life experiences easily, and those who are not willing to accept this suffering and experience in this lifetime create resistance towards their life and suffer even more. So, when you create the resistance of non-acceptance, life becomes more miserable. Since you are putting off a lot of expectations of how your life has to be and how it should be in a particular space and time.

Your inner self always insists you not to go against the creation because it creates a greater problem, which makes life more hectic, and you will not have any interest in life.

Just set everything apart and rest yourself so that the words of your intuition (inner self) can be heard thoroughly. It is your guiding map. Most of the time, we go against our inner selves since we feel that we are making some wrong decisions in our life situations. We always know how our life should be and how others have to live, believing that this is the real and a proper way of living life. Every individual has always misinterpreted life that is actually happening in this world as their reality. Apart from this there is nothing to understand.

But actually, are we living this precious life properly? Are we not doomed in an artificial stage of life? The absence of realisation of humans, towards the awareness of life we are living has created such a huge artificial illusion of life, where we are manifesting again and again the world of illusion to a very large extent. We are dumped into this unrealistic life not knowing the real part, which is struggling to reach you.

But you refuse to trust yourself because you think that you are not good enough, a failure, misery, etc. All those unwanted things have been updated into your mind so that you would not come out of this drama world. As well as you have even started holding this unrealistic life so tightly out of fear, thinking that even if you slightly loosen your grip, you will lose all that you have gathered so far in this life.

You are the powerful genie who can create your own universe with all the goodness, pleasantness and wonderfulness that you always wished to have. For this you have to get detached from this materialistic life and become one with your soul.

Follow the life of love, compassion, truth, happiness and joy to experience the real power within you. You have always been enchanted to live a life of greatness and happiness, but you never got the chance to realise it. Since you're surrounded by this materialistic life, which is always redirecting you from one path to another and not letting you to take the right path of enlightenment.

So better be early to trust yourself than any other thing in life. Since you don't have too much time to realise yourself on this earth. The power of your inner self is to be known to this world so that you can bring others from the dark side of life.

Let's join hands together in oneness with the greater divine energy and enrich the life of others to become the enlightened source of Gods energy, which is waiting for you for a very long period. Hurry up!

Part 3

How Are You Finishing Yourself?
(To Understand)

The Untold Story Of You

"YOU mean I". Nothing to think or nothing to comprehend everything is life within each other. You are the counterpart of me. You have the control over the things I do and even **YOU and I** are the same.

The greater aspect of life is to be understood that everything is interconnected. There is no difference between any human born on this earth, only we humans segregate **YOU and ME.**

Whenever there is mishap or any misunderstanding, you need to wait and take a decision while action is being taken. Everything is attached to everyone. Nothing lives on its own. You have to understand that there are a lot of interconnected chains between each other that are always holding up straight and bonded together. Though we are bonded together, we are individual beings born to display our own life through our own right thoughts.

It has been a part of the life for everyone to bother one another creating another new karma day by day unconsciously. We are all born on a karmic story that has happened in our past life. But yet there is very little insight to understand nature's law.

You need to have greater divinity as you push yourself in the knowledge of greater understanding. There has been a lot of value for the life you live, but you are the one who is not valuing it at any point.

God's story is to make us play an individual character on this earth to finish up all our karma and finally reach God as mentioned in our destiny. But we live on this earth without greater knowledge or wisdom of consciousness on how and for what purpose we have come to live on this earth.

Each and every one on this earth has a great role to perform in different life situations, in order to resolve our karma unknowingly. Very few people have come to realise that the real you, inside you is living a great life which is really required for a human to live on this earth.

You have been less told and less understood.

What for and why are you here?

What is the reason to do all the activities that are needed to be performed on this earth?

As there is no proper teaching and understanding. It has become a real practice to understand only what you see, feel, speak and think only on this basis. The real you are always trying to come out and tell you the life you are living now is not true. It always keeps calling you to the real world which exists within yourself, so that you can have your happiness to a very greater extent. As you connect and understand the real you, thereafter you will never look for any other external requirement to be used to keep yourself content and happy.

A conscious mind will really help you in this understanding of the real you, as you get deeper and deeper. You need not any external guidance to put a smile on your face when you have a strong feeling of connection with your inner soul.

Good things are told and spoken to you, everyday and every moment by your real self. But our subconscious mind never gives any conscious focus to understand what the real being is trying to speak to you. As you follow the inner you, you start getting a lot of guidance to act upon your life.

There is a successful combination (inner self) which holds you up upright in such a way that there is no requirement for any external assistance in life.

All that your inner self tells you is only the path of goodness. You will be always directed to the path of righteousness to reach the source as soon as possible. Your inner soul is your greatest source of energy than any other thing in this world, which always preoccupied everything in life in order to give you the best life of attaining the Highest Source Energy for a fulfilling life.

When your lifestyle, circumstances, situations, your personal experiences, hinder your inner soul. You need to stop overthinking and chattering in mind in order to bring a greater understanding between you and the inner soul. So, as you slow up your mind, you will get into action of greater connectivity where the inner soul tells and you perform the action.

As it has been a lot to understand, calm your mind by just sitting alone, spending time with yourself or doing meditation. These things will easily connect to your real self, and you can live your life with ease.

You and Me are not different but every energy body is in a network where the energy flows from one way to another. You receive all the good signs of life when you are really connected with the real Source Energy. Every important aspect is happening for you with great deal which brings on bliss, happiness and joy.

Your relationship with yourself is an old existence. It cannot be changed at any cost. You have to learn the way to improve your relationship with yourself through pure love, nothing better than love can improve your life. Learn the way to express your love, to one self unconditionally.

There are no rules or a regulation for the love towards oneself has to be. You can propose to yourself the way you like and can propose any number of times because your inner self loves you unconditionally.

Lots and lots of love are expected from thyself as it's the only expectation, nothing other than love. Even though you don't show real love or enough love, the inner self does not react to you for being on the wrong side. Since it only loves the way you are. It only needs you to be a part of its life. But we humans don't realise the real situation of not knowing that our inner self is always ready to love and care for us unconditionally.

You are always followed by your soul each and every second till you are alive. It is always ready to help you to live the best life in any situation. The greater your love, the greater the connection between you and yourself exists. Your life will be taken care of by your inner self, who will be directing you to take action through the form of intuition.

When you have a great realisation of an intuition your life will become so easy that you need not struggle or strain yourself to take your life to the next step. If you have more understanding of intuition, your life will be better than that you had expected.

But for all the understanding you have to do a lot of inner work to connect to your inner self. Since your soul is always speaking to you in the form of intuition and emotion. You need to have a clear focused mind to catch an intuition and understand what type of thoughts arises inside your mind at every moment. You also need to clear your karma from time to time, to understand your inner soul.

As your karma keeps on vaporising, your attachment and love towards your soul becomes stronger. And you need not to be bothered anymore, about how your future will be. Your soul knows what is good and appropriate for you to lead this birth happily by overcoming all types of circumstances very easily. The soul has more than expected power within itself, whereas we humans are unaware, as well as we don't even provide more opportunity for the soul to perform its role.

It is necessary for each human born on this earth to compulsorily realise -

Why have you taken your birth on this planet?

What is the necessity to dissolve your karmas?

So, whenever there is a realisation of inner self, it is better for you to get greatly connected to yourself. As early as possible it is better for each and every single human to realise that there always exists a SOUL purpose. Every human is born to serve its inner soul instead of doing any external work. You have greater responsibility to serve your soul and that is the reason you were born into this world.

But this realisation or consciousness is not attained by everybody in this world because of their karma which stops them from bringing any awareness in themselves.

Don't enroll yourself into the name of fate since God has given all possibilities to each and every individual; they possess the power to create their own life through their thinking capacity. All possibilities exist within you to make life better and try to reach your soul purpose easily.

The more you are connected with your soul, the easier your life is and also the best way to take your life to the highest level of consciousness.

What Are You - YOU???

Identified with the name, status, fame, place, you have been inevitably stuck with your identity of YOU. You're only aware of yourself only through these different forms of identification that you believe to be real. You have not understood what the real YOU are? How will you realise? When will you identify the reality of your life?

There should be something special or different to take you to the next shift of understanding of the real **YOU**. The reality is **YOU** and that is the only one inside you. Don't search the **YOU** by yourself externally, which is already held inside you.

The inside **YOU,** is always speaking to you and telling you that the real **YOU** is always the old existence of the inside **YOU** for a very long period of time that cannot be calculated or assumed. It is your real soul that is the real **YOU**, living within you as the real self.

But we humans do not have the ability or capacity to understand - Where and Why **"YOU"** exist? People are searching very eagerly about their own identity with different types of humans made identity. The external or false identity, which you are now living is not the true form of yourself. You have really nothing to do with this artificial identity unless you are unaware of it.

Increasing the awareness of your life, will reveal the real **YOU**. When there is existence of a greater awareness in your life you will get to know the life of your purpose "Why you are brought to this earth?" Humans assume themselves in different forms but actually you do not possess any shape, form or labels to stick on with it.

Very slowly humans realise their identity only through awareness, when the karma starts dissolving. Until then humans do not understand the concept of the real **"YOU"** and feel there is no requirement to understand the concept of **"YOU"**.

Once a person comes to greater understanding of his or her own purpose of life spiritually, the human starts to connect to the inner self. This inner self is called by different names **"YOU, SOUL, HIGHER CONSCIOUSNESS"** etc. This real **"YOU"** is the true being that has come to the earth to dissolve all the karma it has caused and has been carrying along with it.

The humans who understand the real **YOU** concept get freedom from all sorts of karma issues and always live a blissful and peaceful life.

Understanding **"YOU"** is really a big thing and the real-life purpose of every human born in this life. It is not me who is going to live this life, but my inner self is going to live this life on this earth as per the karmic schedule it possesses.

So, it is very good for a human to make identification with **"YOU"** in order to live a life free from all unwanted pressure and problems. Get soon to the path of blissfulness and peace by taking an opportunity to understand yourself - **"YOU"**.

Emotions of You

Emotions play a very great role in every human life. It is the purpose building point. Emotions carry their own way of feeling for every different feeling you have. Many emotions when bonded together give reason for a very strong feeling that might sometimes make us happy, blissful or very painful.

Every emotion in our life has a greater importance. There is no comparison between the types of feelings we always have. Emotion is put up with great value, where it can change your life's destiny.

Any human realising the power of their own emotions will try to keep it under their own control since every emotions keep on manifesting in your future life. And your current reality is the past emotions that you had intensely delivered with great feelings to the universe.

Each and every emotion should be very carefully observed. How do we feel today? What type of feelings are the emotions giving us? Every emotion is teaching us, "What type of thoughts are currently running in our mind?" Observing emotions is a great practice, which will benefit you in a lot of goodness in your life.

Emotions are always strongly connected to your inner-self. Your real "YOU" does not love the emotions that do not give good feelings to humans. The real "YOU" always loves the emotions and feelings of goodness, joy, happiness, love and self-worth. The real "YOU" gets connected very easily when your emotions are very good and then the inner self will take you to the next shift of your life.

So, as you understand, the emotions of a feeling are the greatest bondage to your soul, they always speak through the positive emotions. Frequently check what emotions are currently running inside you? If there are bad emotions better immediately shift to a good feeling, so that you will be in a greater joy.

Emotions are the one and only way to speak to your real self. Emotions have a great role to play in changing every human life. But many people are not aware of it and do not believe in all these things. Unconscious humans always use their emotions to show their identity. Good emotions give a very good feeling while it is delivered and make you feel the life of abundance & prosperity.

Usage of Your Emotions

Emotions have a very great role to play in your real-life manifestation. It is the real hero behind your past, present and future life. Your emotions depict each and every moment of your life. Because human life on this earth is full of ups and downs due to the types of emotions an individual carries during any situation.

Mankind is unconscious when embedded with mixed emotions, where they are not much aware to come out and discipline their emotions. Each human must master their own emotions to live a happy and blissful life on this earth. Very few humans' discipline or handle their emotions very properly and live the best life, they want to live.

Living a life with proper emotions and knowing how to handle emotions is the real blessing we get from God because human thoughts manifest only when they are attached with emotions. Humans should learn how to use their emotions and where to use the emotions properly.

Every emotion is not of the same type and it is not in the same frequency, it changes according to one's thoughts. Without emotions no human can survive on this earth. It is compulsory for everyone to become aware of "What type of emotion is running in the mind? How does it feel in their heart?" It really is a game between mind and heart. So, keep a check on your feelings when you express a particular emotion.

Many times, most of the emotions are very low and negative, which always make the humans to have a low and negative mindset throughout the day. When the same thing is repeated every-day, their life gets manifested according to their thoughts and humans fall into the prey of suffering.

Humans have to learn to **MASTER** and **DISCIPLINE** their emotions at a very early stage before the subconscious mind is stuffed with unwanted stories. One who has disciplined thoughts also knows how good their future life would be. They learn and also handle not only their own life well they also start to handle other people's life. So, no human can be alive without any emotions. No thoughts manifest without any feelings. It is better to handle emotions and feelings together, slowly. As you repeat the practice you get the habit of being disciplined in your emotions and you will know **"How good life has become"** by mastering emotions.

Emotions, feelings and thoughts, these three are the ingredients of your life source. Respect them, handle them and master them in order to have a blissful life.

Be A Leader In Your Emotions

Your emotions always make you a slave to the life you are living. Nothing else can change your life until you decide to be a leader of your emotions. You need to be the dominant part in handling emotions but it is necessary for you to put your emotions together in such a way that you are able to handle it equally.

Let there be any emotions that arise through your thoughts, you only need to feel and observe it. Don't give any importance to the emotions that do not bring fruitfulness to your life. You need to handle it in such a way that there is no differentiation with any feelings that create good or bad emotions. All emotions are embodied into your mind without any conditional restriction.

As you gradually get used to emotions, you will realise how easy your life has become. From the start of your life to the end you are bound to experience emotions. So, it should be better for you to take care of the emotions that are flowing into your mind and the situation you are living in.

As you live a particular lifestyle, you also have a particular emotion to go with. According to your situation or your lifestyle, your emotions also differ since your life is connected to your thoughts and where the thoughts give the feeling of emotions. At this particular time, you need to decide whether to give importance or to react to it. So, when human becomes a leader to handle one's emotion, life becomes easy and sturdy to live. Managing emotion is the greatest skill for each and everyone. It is not said that you need to hide or control your thoughts. It is to be understood as to which emotion should be given importance and which one should not.

As you slowly master your emotions your life will come to an understanding of how each and every moment of life is working for you and how you are creating the reality of life.

So, it is compulsory to be a leader in handling your thoughts, with any type of practice that will make your life necessarily wonderful. Learn to handle this great life that God has gifted you, as you deserve to live with happiness and joy.

Willingness To Live The Life You Want To Live

How have you been living all these days? I am sure that there is a lot of confusion still running in your mind, even though you believe that you have a very better life than anybody else.

Yes! It is not to be misunderstood that people always believe that they are living the life they want, but in certain cases, most people are dissatisfied because of the comparative mind and not feeling contented, even in most of the situations when everything is displayed in front of them.

Good thoughts, good attitude and a good life are always added to your survival skills, in order to live the life you want. When most of the people on the earth are struggling with the life they want to live, some are not even bothered about - What type of life are they living? They think that life has to be taken as it flows. There is always a phrase **"Go with the flow"**, it is true but it is meant to, accept that moment and try to live with what is really required. But most of us do not realise that we need to take a particular action for that particular moment. As we always assume that life comes with suffering and only lucky people are meant to live this life happily, actually it does not work that way.

No human is lucky on this earth, only their own actions, thoughts and karma influence all the luck for their life. Every human has to understand that God did not send us to undergo struggle or suffer this beautiful life but only human over thinking has led to suffering. Because we humans fear the past and future and don't have the guts to live the present moment, believing that we will lose the chance of the past and future moments.

Don't always pressurise yourself so much, whatever is meant to happen will always happen. You have to believe that every human born on this earth have something to do with their own lives. The purpose of life has got them to this place, in order to show for what reason they are here and why have they taken birth as humans on this earth?

Humans must evolve to understand the birth and death of their life and analyse, what is this birth telling them as well as why are we all born as humans, particularly on the earth? So, it is a very great and a large subject to understand but every single human of any age, has to understand that it is something essential to realise before life ends.

When individual take steps to learn about their life purpose, a lot of mysteries open up to them. No human needs to get frightened and feel that it's unbelievable for everything that unfolds in front of them.

As humans come to know, this physical body or this materialistic life is making them live on the planet is only an illusion, and they really have nothing to do with it. Humans and all the things that exist around us are full of energy and everything is made of energy. Only we humans consider and segregate living and non-living beings, but anything that you see and everything that you don't see is energy, and that is vibrating in its own frequency.

When you actually come to an understanding that everything is energy, you will gradually realise that there is nothing to feel and even think about the life you are actually living. Along with energy, karmic accounts always play a very great role.

This karma not only creates the life you live but also makes you take action for, what you have to perform on this earth. So, life is full of karmic accounts and energy frequency which make the solid physical body perform survival skills on this earth. This is how a human life is designed, where your good thoughts and good actions will try to make your life better and improved for every birth you take on this earth.

Pushing your life from one birth, to another birth, not even knowing why we all are here on this planet makes human life more miserable.

I feel very bad and feel sorry for the suffering they are undergoing without any understanding of their living. Let every human get a chance to know their life's purpose as early as possible, at least in this birth before their life ceases, so that they can prioritise it and live life to become a pure soul and reach their source energy.

Reincarnation or rebirth, everything has a great connection between one person's death and birth. It is valuable for the moment of life you are living in. But many humans indulge in this artificial, illusion life never knowing how much they are missing the birth value as humans, on this planet.

When every human gets to know the reason, why they are here, they will become aware of their life and would be conscious of their inner self.

Happy To Live This Life?

When do you realise that goodness is happening in this life? Great beginnings always give you a new birth into this life. You experience a rebirth twice when you understand this reality of life. So many changes, so much of realisation does not happen all of a sudden. It is a great blessing for that to happen in your life when the higher consciousness chooses you. But many are confused about **"What kind of a realisation is really required for living a happy life?"**

Let me brief you, when everyone born on this earth wants a life of love, joy and happiness. But have doubts - How can I get it with my understanding? Do I need to struggle or do any hard work? Not much to think, we are all blessed to live the life we want to live with a lot of abundance and prosperity. There is not a limitation for any good thing. Humans, the children of God, are blessed to be limitless. Neither good, nor bad in this world has no meaning until and unless you understand, what is really required or what you want in this life?

There is a lot much you need to know, why is life like a secret not making us understand the real meaning? Yes, human life is full of miracles and amusement. When it is openly revealed, no humans are really accepting the fact of reality because we have been living a meaningless and a materialistic life. So, it has become a difficult task to know the reality and authenticity of life.

Everyone has the right to live life by connecting with the source which is always residing within you. Your inner self is the source of all your happiness, greatness and goodness for your survival on this earth.

Many righteous paths always exist within you, to live the life of consciousness and awareness. Mind does not allow us to understand which path we are actually travelling on.

Since our inner self is shouting badly, at least some time we will understand that someone is really trying to help us with our life. It is better for every human being to come down from all the work that they are doing and take up silence and patience, to hear the inner voice that is always speaking to them.

As you and your soul become one person, life becomes so easy and happy, and you need not strain yourself for anything because it starts thinking on your behalf. It starts to tell you where to stop and where to start. Really surprising! How is it possible for such a wonderful thing to live with such a higher consciousness that knows what is good for you?

But do you think you need to be idle throughout your life, when someone is thinking about you. It is not in that sense; you keep doing all the things that make you feel like you are moving on the right path. As you think and take action with your little understanding, your inner self keeps on supporting and directing you in which way your life has to be.

Your inner self has only one goal to make your life full of joy, happiness and goodness. And also make you attain the purpose of your life. So, when your inner self takes so much responsibility for keeping you alive for a life of peace, consciousness, joy and happiness, your life becomes blissful.

You are born only to live life with happiness and the only person, who is willing and working to make your life blissful is your SOUL. The soul lives for you, acts for you and takes the total responsibility of your life.

It is such a wonderful life when one is ready to take the whole responsibility of your life from your birth to death. So, living life happily on the earth is the easiest process of any other thing in this world, but only when you understand your soul's purpose with full awareness and consciousness.

"Dear people, live a life full of love, happiness, peace and greatness to every extent so that even your bad Karma will dissolve in such a way that it has nothing to do in future for you".

You Have Been Teleported

A life with a beautiful journey would always exist in everybody's life, when you allow life to happen in its own way. Yes, this beautiful life has always been enriched with all uniqueness of greatness, from every small to large thing. You have been designed always to live a life of happiness, joy and goodness. What are the humans always waiting for? Don't know? Actually, NO! Humans don't know what actually and specifically they need. Since the desire is changing moment after moment. In case you hold a desire, you become very desperate to manifest it immediately according to your own timing.

There have been a lot of searches for - What this human life has to do with? Are we the only beings having this type of system of living? Does it not feel very awestruck? Hey, what is really happening here? Not knowing answers for such a lot of things always puts us in amusement.

What type of creation are we living? Why is this human mind and body undergoing so much change? Is it an external or an internal factor creating and executing our life? Why are all these things actually happening?

Now as we have come to a stage of realisation that something is happening to us each and every moment in our mind, body, and soul, many questions arises in mind: Why is it so? What type of being have we been to do this human life on this planet? Only we are the creatures existing or do we have someone living along with us who cannot be felt and seen?

Many researchers and great Guru's provide a lot of much information that they have gathered from this huge universe. Really it is such an unbelievable thing, we have always been teleported from one universe to another universe, from one planet to another planet and many more which is unexplainable.

Feeling surprised, yes, we all should be astonished to know that we are being teleported from birth to death, each day and every day.

Yes! Every night in your sleep, your soul is teleported from one place to another place, where you are not able to remember and understand the happenings. Your birth and death take place in a different place, and again, the next birth takes place in another place. Nobody, even you cannot decide where and what can happen to you while you sleep, as well as where you should be born and where you die.

There is a very large existence, which is beyond our imagination, where we do not realise the dimension, we are living in. Everything in this existence is always teleporting itself from one form to another form and from one place to another place. Are we humans actually aware of this happening? Very few people have gathered this type of information consciously to understand their life's existence.

In every part of this multiple universe, there is always teleportation of lives and unknown matter from time to time, which is beyond our understanding. Many lives have been teleported easily in their known ways, where it makes us think that everything is unbelievable. Be aware of each and every moment of our life, that even our thoughts are being teleported from one being to another being (aliens) which is actually not understood by normal human lives.

Since something is not in our understanding and cannot be seen, it is never meant to exist or happen. A greater network of energy is working beyond our life, for everything to happen across this universe. Where is our understanding in this case? Only the absence of awareness and consciousness does not meet the realisation of life.

Most beings of life suffering from unconscious living should try to get out of this messed up entanglement of non-understanding life. Otherwise, you would be caught up only in the play of life and death. Understand you are the actual being of this universe, in the form of a soul surviving in your own existence.

You Are A Treasure Box

As you know, life is always full of surprises in its own way. Miracles always keep happening at every edge of life even without understanding. Why is it happening? Life has always given beautiful returns to make humans realise - How important they are and what all is life always ready to give?

As you prefer to live this life you keep getting things you need. There is always an abundance of opportunities and gifts available in front of you but there is a lack of realisation that everything in life is lying before us. Whenever you look out for a particular thing you require, it always exists.

Every part of life is telling us something new but we humans with an unconscious mind never look through it. Only your consciousness is the tool which will tell you what is going around you. You actually do not need to steer yourself very hard but one thing you must do is to be aware of every moment that you live. It seems and it is very difficult to be so, only after practice you can achieve this consciousness.

What is the purpose of me being conscious?

Why so? What is the benefit I acquire through it?

Such a lot of questions, but to your amazement you will get the answers when you are very aware.

Yes! Awareness always briefs you, what is really happening to your life and what role you play in your life. Isn't it nice to know what I am doing in my life? Don't calculate your salary, status, family and so on. This is not something you need to understand.

What is your part as a being on this earth you have been doing? That means you are a human being dressed up on this earth to perform a particular act. To easily understand you are the powerful soul particle vibrating in a particular frequency to match the universal vibration in different ways.

As you realise you are not what you think. You are your **SOUL**, the reality of being on this earth. Your **SOUL** is more powerful than you think. Its power cannot be measured to any extent because humans might be genius or intelligent, but we are always limited to the power of thinking. There is always a very powerful existence on this earth which you cannot imagine.

The **SOUL** is so extraordinarily powerful within each one of us, you need not struggle with this existing life to live on this earth. Because your **SOUL** knows everything perfectly, it knows how and when an individual has to get awakened.

You humans do not understand how powerful each of you are since there is the **SOUL** existence that has a brief answer to your life. If you wish to achieve and change your life for betterment, just get connected to the inner being **(SOUL)**. No other than your **SOUL**, can reveal that treasure you hold in your life.

Your **SOUL** has so much power and that is limitless, it is your guidance, path changer, uplifter, reality of purpose and your revealer of answer to every question, and so on. There are no words to explain the magnificent power it has. There is everything in your **SOUL**. Only one thing you need to do now is to get connected to your **SOUL**, it might be difficult initially. For some people, connecting to their inner selves might be very easy but for many, it is most difficult and oblivious. All the work is only based upon your karma.

Karma plays an all-time role in structuring your life at every step you take. Karma knows when you will be able to connect to your inner self and will come out of this illusionary life. It is better for you to dissolve all the karmas and surrender to the **SOUL**, which is the greatest treasure box for your happy living on this earth.

Do understand you (SOUL) are the treasure box of your life don't keep searching for it externally as it already exists within you. Dig it out as quickly as possible and just connect to your inner being and then you will see magic happening in your life. You are a treasure, handle it wisely and awaken your life to live blissfully.

Are You Tolerating At Your Heart Level?

"Your heart is your pacemaker - creates and makes life more beautiful as expected in unexpected surprise".

As you have thought and imagined life always seems to be difficult since our mind is conditioned in that way and there is nothing to blame ourselves or others. Life is full of ups and downs and goes round and round with the same repetitions and pains. Okay, let us stop here itself what is that one thing that makes you feel better every time you are in a low mood? Something would have helped you to bring back your mood as usual. What can it be? No idea.

When you are feeling low or are in an improving situation, there is always a contradictional fight between your mind and heart. You would have felt deeply but not realised. Does your heart listen to the mind? No, never at all! But it works vice versa. Your mind changes when your heart feelings change. You can feel pain in your heart since your heart reflects all pains and emotions at every level. But the mind does not. A mind only brings a type of thought as you think, it can be related or the other side. But thoughts bring emotional feelings which are felt within the heart. Your heart actually reacts to the emotions of thoughts, you have brought into your mind.

Your heart's emotions make it easy for you to catch, the type of thought that is flowing into mind and even you realise, what you are thinking?

Happy emotions - Happy thoughts

Uneasy emotions - Unwanted thoughts

When you are easily in the habit of catching your feelings, you will learn to become aware of your thoughts. As you become more and more conscious of the thoughts that are flowing into your mind, you will realise what you are thinking. When identification of thoughts comes easily with the heart feelings, then life becomes easy in such a way, that each and every moment of life starts improving and good things start to manifest as you had wished.

Understand that the heart has a very, very important role to make your life easier and beautiful. Not only that, but it helps you to become more conscious and aware of your life, and very easily, you will start deleting and removing unwanted thoughts that are not actually needed at all.

Whenever you have a heart ache, you feel pain and somewhat uneasiness, which makes sure that some improper thought is running in your head. Don't take your heart's feelings for granted as feelings keep changing every second. We cannot catch hold of every thought in life. But wherever possible listen to your heart's feelings, which are filled with full of good and bad emotions. So, how to be always aware of your thoughts? As we carry more than 60,000 thoughts every day. It looks hectic, but it is real. When practiced consciously, your inner self starts providing all the support you always needed, and your intuition will guide you in the right way that no one knows. So as your consciousness is at highest peak, your inner self takes accountability to your life and tries to lead you in the correct way which you are meant to travel on.

It would be better if everyone in life learns to live life from the heart rather than the mind. Mind plays both the good side and the other side of life even without any realisation because the mind does not know how to think. Only we humans can train it up in such a way that life becomes more blissful.

Put your heart feelings in front of every situation you face in life and take strong necessary steps as your intuition tells you. You do not need any second thoughts to doubt your intuition because the intuition always arises from your feelings. Make sure you do everything in the proper way for your life but for others it may not be right. Just don't bother too much in life telling and explaining everything to every person. People will only understand what they want to understand.

So, don't struggle with yourself to satisfy other people's needs and expectations because minds always keep changing and they do not know what they themselves are doing for their own life.

Live life of happiness with your heart's feelings, each and every second in every different way with respect to the thought you absorb.

Great Value Of Life

"Don't search for any greatest support externally when everything exists internally, self-sufficiently, powerfully and magnificently".

What is a great value of life? Do you have any idea how to find it out? No! Everyone consider the things (you hold) that are currently adding value to life as the greatest value in their life. Some might consider money, status, home, family, job and many more. The list of valuable things that we hold in life might seem very important but actually all that you hold very tightly is an illusion. You are holding, which is not real.

I know you people might think - Whatever I hold gives me emotion, sentiment, happiness and also feelings that make me feel better. Not only so, you have the greatest relationship with all the illusion realities. Since you find everything to be good enough to make life somewhat satisfied. There is nothing wrong to have some attachment, but when you indulge your life so hopefully with things around you, you are really building your life. But we humans never realise and come to an understanding that something really very valuable is existing here.

As you proclaim that everything on earth is an illusion of reality through some little understanding and knowledge, your life starts to shift from one level to another. Since this little realisation will take you to another dimension of life, you will understand that for so many days, you have been wasting time on useless things that are not really the source of life.

Okay, what would be your real understanding? Your real-life values come from within you. Yes, to specifically understand the great value of your life is within each one of us. It is none other than anyone else - **your POWERFUL SOUL.**

Many don't realise the greatest value and power this soul holds because we are not able to identify with our unconscious mind. Being born as human is the greatest advantage we have received in our life. In this greatest advantage we humans hold the powerful source of energy - **SOUL**.

We might call our inner soul with different names but the power and magnificence it has, is not explainable. Your inner soul is always trying to pull you inward within yourself. Even though, throughout life you keep on searching everything externally to understand life, nothing like your inner self can be achieved.

Do understand that every happening of life starts within you. When slowly you start observing how you are, what is really happening to you in each aspect of your life? You little understand that there exists a strong internal force that is trying and pushing hard to reach you non - physically. This inner force does not have any physical existence but whatever miracles it brings out in your life are displayed in physical form. Showing your inward reflection externally as you have understood and realised gives the result that you wish to happen. As you stimulate the feeling within your inner self, something greater than life starts to happen so powerfully that you have not expected.

You, yourself get astonished by the things happening around you. Am I doing all these things? Because we humans have always survived on physical proof and when abnormal to your understanding starts to take place we can't believe.

The inner source power is so high, that even you cannot calculate or imagine how this powerful being is working with such enormous energy and putting everything in the right place. We might be thinking that we do not have any talent to prove ourselves, but this powerful energy source brings out the magnificent energy of all creativity and action, which will change your life drastically that you will be in an unexplainable situation.

You always think whatever you learn or do is only the result of the present life. But the power, talent, energy and practice, all the things required for your life are carried by thousands of lives you have lived unknowingly. All these things happen unconsciously without any idea that you have. It would be better if you try to connect with your inner self as early as possible to make your life easy, and whatever you had thought would not happen, will be possible.

You are of greater value than any other things in life. Just learn to value, identify and love yourself more than anyone to make your life more blissful than any other thing, you have expected.

Jurisdiction Of Your Life

"Get surrendered to God's law and jurisdiction in order to feel, live a safe and peaceful life".

As you live your life on your own terms and rules you experience a lot of things that are not avoidable. Since you feel that the freedom of life in your way is not disturbing anyone around you. But do we live our life by not impacting others or interfering in anybody's life? You expect that changes should happen to your life miraculously, as you are living your way. Yes, there is nothing wrong to do so but do understand life is always miraculous in each and every moment you exist on this earth.

When there is a level of thought that always dominates your level of behaviour. It would become a major physical action or a circumstance that happens in an unexpected time. So, as you wish to live life in happiness and blissfulness, life starts turning into a situation which bring happiness to your life. You have to realise that life changes, as you change your thoughts and the way you think. Better thoughts always yield a better life especially when you are more aware of your existence. As you keep on planning each and every moment of your life, you don't realise someone above you is creating a major life plan which you are not aware of at all.

Both you and your life are like your two eyes, where you cannot betray anyone to make the other win. Because of yourself and life is - **YOU**. Then what is the necessity for you to worry about anything that even does not exist on this plain. A lot of things in life happen in an unexpected way, where you do not get a chance to even imagine things in life. Then who is the **"POWER"** that is always creating changes in your life, which is not asking for any of your opinion? We humans have decided to live unconsciously, where you start to yield the unknown result, which never goes in your own way. But have you struggled enough to know, who is taking all the jurisdiction of life? What is that one power creating everything in a single unique jurisdiction law of universe? No idea, where do all these things exist? But in every state of life, you start getting the jurisdiction law of the universe to reflect on you.

You should clearly understand that there is a legal system to run this country. There even exists the law of universe, where law cannot be taken into your hand or cannot bribe anyone. Because you are not aware which universe's law will be creating which judgement. In the court of God's jurisdiction, there never exists things like good or bad, high or low; it can be anything. The law of God is only your karma. Karma is segregated on good or bad acts. Even when the universal god takes any action very strongly, it only triggers its power on the karma you have made and will be making.

In God's jurisdiction there is no attachment to anything but only it looks for the actions that you have performed all these years. Your divine God's action is always unexpected because we think if we do only good actions, we would get good karma but another person with a lot of positive thinking, might be facing big punishments, insults etc. Since your life is only working below god's jurisdiction, where there does not exist any rule.

The universal law and rules are only understood by the greater higher self whose action is unexplainable and unimaginable. So dear humans, always be careful with your life. Every moment that you live your life you are always giving way for god's rules to happen successfully.

The way you are conscious and aware of life, it will always lead you to the greater level of living with the blessings of God and every time God is always working in its power of law.

To make your life more efficient, it is possible only through you and your belief system, which throws a force of life power, in order to make your life a better place to live and exist.

Mistakes Of Life

"Great consciousness of life flows like a river of wisdom which is not restricted to any rules of your understanding".

Mistakes are always meant to be part of our life. No humans survive only on their righteous path. Life is filled with energies that can harm and disrupt our structure of life. But we humans have learnt to handle our life in such a way we are ready to hurt ourselves to escape the situation of misery and suffering. Great blessings always happen in a massive scale but lack of realisation by the humanity leads to worries and griefs.

You have been always led towards a life of goodness, each and every moment, even though you consciously keep on making mistakes but the divine energy within you is always trying to give the best part of the situation. Since, we humans have a lot of expectations and create our own reality we do not allow God or divine interference to take place in our life.

So as life goes on and on you have become so hard and difficult, you have no time to look into your family, where the existence of happiness and liveliness is in absence. We have not realised the mistakes that are ruling our life from birth to death. It has become a part of life to consider mistakes as casual activities. Yes, it can be a casual activity but when you lose your consciousness the life you live becomes more miserable. Hence you find it difficult to overcome and blame God and others for the miserable life you are living.

The mistakes of life always bring karma in every action that you do. The good or bad whatever you perform, is on the basis of karma that you have executed in your past life. The second nature of life is your co-creation and the first part would be displayed by karma. As you come across a lot of circumstances of goodness, you feel blessed by the divine but when something does not go your way, you are ready to curse the divine which created this situation of suffering. Every creation is always your part of the action that you have always created.

Make sure that each and every day life happens in the best way up to your understanding. You need a lot of awareness to understand, what is actually happening to you. Have you ever felt that something great is always flowing into your life process? And do understand that only the best part is happening to you what you are not aware of.

Then the question arises how can I make my life easier? In what way would I feel better? So, the question starts to hang around you. You start understanding that you have started checking your life and you are aware that something great is happening in the present moment you are living. Yes! Great, this is the first step of realisation that you looked upon yourself for the betterment of living. Here comes the beginning of goodness in your life, where all your bad karmas have started dissolving. At this point, you need to know that something very powerful and unexpected miracles are going to happen each and every day with the help of your conscious awareness. This is how your life gets transformed without your help. Everything becomes unbelievable, when life turns its good side to you.

Making a mistake does not make you small and indifferent. But when you know that you have created the mistake that has manifested in your life. For the person who takes responsibility for each and every action of life, life flows easily and you become more conscious of the type of life you are living.

Every great realisation of human beings always gives birth to the better shift in life of every being on this earth. Humans have a very great chance to understand and take responsibility for the life they have created with all goodness and mistakes.

Understand dear ones great mistakes always have resulted in great achievements, which is above all the understanding of our earthly consciousness.

Never control yourself from being the child of the divine world. Here you have to learn from the mistakes you have made and get enlightened by the wisdom you have possessed. Everything you do and perform is a great happening in itself, creating a new life. So be happy to live life with the greatness of wonders, which is always creating miracles of life.

"Be alive and be a life for yourself".

Making Of The Universe

"You are the universe, and you will be the universe - Only for your existence".

Have you ever thought of being a Universe? Why? You never felt it or never knew about the universe. Let it be anything but you should have felt and realised, how many times that something unknown is always working behind you. You might have felt it but lack of understanding or having no time spent on realising that did not help you acknowledge.

There is always something miraculous, unexpected events are always taking place without our knowledge. Even when you realise, you don't give so much importance to thinking and believing that it has to happen, it is happening. But do understand, there is a very strong force working behind it. This divine force does not have any physical form or structure to identify. Also, it never likes someone to identify with a particular thing. Since this special force is not in the fixed form, it is unexplainable and above all it is human thinking.

Great things always attempt to bring something special in life, which is not assumed or imagined by the normal human brain. There is always a creation happening each and every second of life, where humans fail to understand and observe that things are being created again and again.

As usual, you are always living life that is uneasy and also not favourable for your living condition but have you stopped for a moment to think, what really is happening? What am I doing? Am I working in a situation that is favourable for my life? There is nothing wrong with thinking for your betterment because understand that you are very important in your life apart from anything. If one does not see purpose in their existence, why would they choose to continue living this life? Learn to understand yourself since there lives a very larger existence, which cannot be seen and it exists more powerful than expected.

You will have to expect a great understanding when you realise your life system. What is this existence not having any physical form but more powerful than any other thing? Are you astonished? There's nothing other than the SOUL - The universe of your life.

You might feel stupid after knowing that a mini universe exists within humans. Is it to be believed? How can such a big existence of the external world be stuffed into one physical body, who did this? Such a lot of questions arise from not knowing. What is it?

Do understand that the great existence of this universe is in a miniature form in the physical body. It undergoes all the changes as the universe experiences. So only we are able to get connected to the cosmos energy very easily, not even doing any particular action to be in constant connection with the higher energy.

As you have accepted the universe's existence within you, you get to experience all the changes and different forms of life understanding by yourself. You will get more connected to the universe. This understanding makes you feel more reliable to live this life (the universe within you and the external).

You have been always connected to this universal world so start making your own universe. Making the universe is not physical, but creating your own life terms from the wisdom that you have achieved will help you start to make a new universe for yourself in order to experience and dissolve within it. Hence you are the universe.

You are the existence of physical form and you are the co-creator of your own life under the guidance of the higher energy source. As you make your universe a place to live a peaceful and compassionate life, there is always support and protection provided to you at each and every moment till you exist on this earth.

Development Of Thoughts

"Thoughts always flow but you are the maker of your life with consciousness and awareness."

As you use your mind to think, you will learn to generate a thought of its own kind. Thoughts flow cannot be controlled and what type of thoughts should flow also cannot be controlled. Thoughts are like air which cannot be stopped in any aspect of life. You may think practicing any type of activities might control the flow of thoughts but it's really impossible. **It is as it is.**

We humans never create any thoughts that we like. We only think about the way we want them in our life, and then related to it sometimes, the thought flows. Who made this thought? Why does it keep on flowing? Is it necessary to have it? Such a lot of questions keep on coming in our mind non-stop, not knowing what to do. As you think thoughts are related but sometimes that's not much related. Most of the time the generation of thoughts is really not related, it appears on its own wish. Only we humans have to learn to be out of the thoughts that are flowing into our mind. More consciousness is required to handle our thoughts.

Life is full of goodness, when we become more conscious and aware of what we are into. Since human life is so busy, sometimes more critical than expected and unscheduled, where we never find time to be conscious of what we are thinking. You need not find any separate time to be conscious of thoughts. It is just a daily required practice, where you have to make it compulsory, to be conscious of what you are thinking. You have no other choice better than this to make life more beautiful.

Practice, practice throughout your lifetime, because only your thoughts are creating your life, nothing more than that. Understand, only thoughts can change your life, nothing else in life will change your thoughts.

In real life, we need a lot of conscious thinking so that we will be able to yield conscious situations, as the thoughts flow. Thoughts are uncontrollable. You should learn to master yourself in such a way that you must know which thought is to be yielded and which thought to be pushed away from life.

Lot of mind consciousness is required for practicing consciousness. It is not a very easy matter but as you practice, you will easily take charge of your thoughts.

You cannot decide what type of thoughts will flow and what not because you are not the creator of your thoughts, and you cannot even identify from where it flows. But one thing is confirmed that without the knowledge of the higher energy source nothing is happening. Only a creator is incharge of our thoughts. No human has still identified, where these thoughts come from.

Can any science explain it because we have no proof to show the way it is generating thoughts. Thoughts immediately flow into the human mind, as soon as you are born. It is a miracle as something wanted and unwanted is flowing into a mind knowingly and unknowingly.

We have our life based only upon our thoughts and realise how much responsibility we have. Everything starts from your thoughts. When your thoughts are given life with emotion and feelings you generate another life thought without knowing whether it is good or bad. Life starts happening due to the thoughts which you have given importance and start getting manifested into the reality of your life.

So, what can be done, that our life becomes better and we live the best life? **Be conscious.** Slow down the thinking of your mind. Don't be in a hurry, so that you never have a chance to look into your life.

Stop over thinking and concentrate on each and every moment that is meant to tell you to be in the present moment. That is the only choice when you want to take care of your thoughts.

As you learn to be in the present moment, you will become a master of thoughts and you will understand how to add feelings and emotions, to generate another life situation that is really needed.

How Are You Willing To Live This Life?

"Being with soul connection is life to all connections of understanding and belief in life".

How are you willing to live this life? As usual, as same as everybody is living their life. It always seems good to me and you, to lead a regular life as all humans are usually leading their life. Does everyone have the same life span, style, attitude, behaviour and status or some other thing? Then why should we have to live the same type of life of struggle, happiness, pain, fear, guilt, joy etc. Do we not need a filter to have a unique life apart from everybody? We assume that being unique means being in a particular career, having a very high status and so on. Because we have lived in this type of a society, that segregates people's life on success and failure. We also believe that we have to strive very hard to live this life of success and show proof to the people around us.

The whole lot of the population on this divine earth is only struggling to be happy and successful in every part of life. So that they will get approval and validity in the society they are living.

Since we are born on this earth, people are discriminated and separated by a large set of issues that humans have decided themselves. There are so many identities we live with, that we cannot escape at all. It might be rich, a poor status, caste, creed, religion, dark, fair anything, there are such a lot of things which cannot be named. Human life has become so complicated due to narrow thinking. We all humans born on this earth are handcuffed by ourselves, with all the unconscious thoughts and beliefs which we have been fed with throughout our lifetime. This knowledge and idea is held up in the life of struggle and pain, which is always accepted by human beings that we are always going to suffer without understanding the purpose of life.

There is nothing to blame anyone, but many people are not willing to come out of the nutshell of pain and suffering, believing they are meant to live this way. How many are willing to live a life out of all the understanding that you learnt at your young age? Actually, this is not your real life. We have to push ourselves somewhere or the other so hard that life puts us in such a situation where you understand that you have to come to live the life of your purpose, to serve and help people around you.

First you have to heal your own self. Healing is a very great term of realisation, to come out of an unrealistic life of fear, guilt, pain, attachments, past and future, which all you now believe as reality. It is all engulfed into the illusion of unrealistic realisation.

You would really feel amazed to know - Am I living a life of illusion or maya? It is the life of nothingness from birth to death, struggling to sustain this illusion life with such a lot of unfairness and foolishness that each and every human body is undergoing. When the actual realisation happens about oneself you will always stand apart from the population of unconscious living.

The person with great realisation of belief and understanding of their own life will become more conscious and aware. Every moment of life will become very easy to live and you will start understanding that true happiness lies in the present moment you live. When there comes awareness to play your **SOUL** - Divineness living inside you starts shining so brightly, you will start to be in its brightness and follow the inner guidance without any second thought.

The connection between you and your **SOUL** is such a blessing. Without God's or Higher Source's blessing nothing is happening in your life. You get held by **GOD - SOUL** which will lead you to the path of greater understanding to reach the destination of light - **ENLIGHTENMENT**.

It feels so amazing when you read these types of lines of **BLESSINGS, GOD, SOUL, ENLIGHTENMENT** and so on. You have to take your own time to make yourself better at each and every part of the moment you live. Do not procrastinate in the mind's belief. Once connected to your soul, just surrender and the path to enlightenment is ready for you.

You Are Destined

What you are to be, you always are. Actually, our life seems confusing. We feel a very great connection with the work that is in the process along with life but not in real connection. We seem to live a life of non-effective syndrome, thinking that we are building a life successfully by going to work and taking responsibilities. But in reality it does not seem so. There are a lot of struggles in each and every aspect of life and that is hindering our growth to the other level. Why do we have to live this hectic life which is also full of miseries and non-understanding? Only confusion and struggles are holding all life jobs.

Are we sure life is making it difficult to live a simple life? Since we keep on comparing ourselves with others status or personalities in other aspects of life. We tend to live a life without proper understanding. We have assumed that life is full of circles: born, get educated, take a job, get married, have kids and finally die. But dear humans understand that the reality of life is not as understood by you. It is all human made life, not letting anyone to get rid of this karmic life cycle.

Do understand that the life we live is full of entanglement. You have not come here to get married and only reproduce. You have come to dissolve all your karma. Realise that living a regular life has nothing to do with you, until you become more conscious. You need to get awareness of life and become more conscious. Why are you living this type of life? Why have we come to this earth? Do we just come here to be born and die in repeated cycles? No, no, not at all, it is a wrong understanding, actually you have taken this birth to dissolve all your karma through different stages of life and finally get connected to your higher source.

Many don't have knowledge of the highest source but we pray daily, asking **GOD** to help us and get us out of all sufferings. Even though we pray daily, have we seen or either felt **GOD. GOD** is a feeling source. It can be only felt when realised with your own awareness. It is some sort of higher power source which cannot be seen with your normal eyes. It is a superpower energy, which can be acquired through your wisdom. Your wisdom makes you understand that the **GOD'S** energy, always resides inside you and as well as in this universe.

There is no place without the existence of the higher source - **GOD**. Nothing can be created with the absence of **GOD** in this universe. You need to understand that there is a Highest Source of Energy, that has created you and everything in this world and that is needed for you.

You have to understand that your creator - **GOD** has already destined you for the type of life you have to live in this birth. You cannot change your destination. Even if you are trying to manipulate your life and create your own life, you have to undergo all the sufferings and goodness for all the things you have created. Whatever it might be, the end result will be the creator's destiny for you. You may take any path as you wish since you are the co-creator of life. But in the end, only the god's destined life will only prosper for you.

You think that you have planned and created every step of life but in reality, you are living out of the karmic section of your past life.

You are destined by your creator. Only your creator knows your destination but humans struggle so much to survive on this earth. Everything is handled by the highest power; you have to only dance to the god's creation. So better you get prepared and understand to live a life of consciousness and happiness. Thank you

Be a child of God. You are always blessed - You are destined.

New Life Time Process

"Your knowledge of association with the greater wisdom of life will give you all the answers of life".

As you start to live the life of your choice, you never understand where to start and where to stop. Since earlier you were always guided through some community and family beliefs but now none will come to play. There will be a very big open space to think and recreate your life. You know, you have taken a new journey in your personal life, which will have a lot of confusions and engagements, putting you into different levels of realisation. You will do all new things that help you in the betterment of your life.

Taking a very big leap of change for an individual is such a great courage that a human possesses and which will bring all the changes of known and unknown things. But you have to build a path in such a way of not making a mistake of going back to the old life of misery, guilt, fear and many more, that has just stopped you far behind from taking away your awareness and consciousness of life.

As the realisation of each individual builds up, you will start searching for different meanings of life to evaluate what is happening around you. You will find something more interesting, about the life that you are about to live.

Start your life out of consciousness, of what is going on each and every time because you are meant to live every moment, where miracles are happening again and again. Every moment is trying to bring new life in each and every process of life. But you are denying yourself by keeping yourself engaged within unrealistic, materialistic life. You have to deepen your senses of thinking without doubting yourself.

Every edge of life is giving you a new wisdom telling that you are not a human to suffer the pain of life. The living of life comes with the finishing up of your soul purpose, of what you have come here to do. Get to know the purpose of living on this Earth. What related actions have you performed so far to know the reason? Why have you stepped on this earth? So come to an understanding that you are such a special being, that the creator has brought you to this earth, with a purpose to deliver a particular action. Your actions or performance should be helpful for others, but instead we are not living such a life. We are eager to make ourselves richer, more materialistic with all the comforts and luxury. Even though we possess all, we don't stop at a particular point. Because we have become the slave of money, luxury, fame, status which is riding a roller coaster game that never makes us go high nor lets us go down.

You need to understand, when you can get everything through your richness, why not peace and happiness a possibility? Then, there should be another life process which should give you peace, without even spending a penny.

Love and peace are that requirements of every human being but they don't know how to get it easily. Only the realisation of self will help you to understand the purpose of your life. You have to be guided towards awareness and consciousness understanding. You are just a tool of your greatest creation; you have nothing to perform of your own. Everything is destined and designed in such a way that you attain and take the path of enlightenment.

Nothing more has to be performed on this earth. Only the realisation of self is the ultimate goal of your life. As you understand this reality, changes happen to you. You are existing for every situation of your life, by taking the responsibility that everything is meant to happen for a reason. Just process the new life with your guided soul and let go of all the pain, sufferings and a fearful life.

Your new life process will tell you how to keep yourself engaged in this new life with a lot of awareness and consciousness. And you will start to believe that each and every action you are creating is already created. Nothing new is there to be performed, and your only purpose is to bring out the real you into life which is abundantly prosperous, powerful and talented.

Nobody can stop your soul from doing something. Only your awareness gives you a new life of understanding, that you are only an energy body, nothing apart from it. You are here to get rid of unwanted realities and get new life experiences, helping you to dissolve all the karma. As your karma dissolves and is neutralized, you go back to your greater oneness which is your home destiny, from where you came. **You have to return back.**

The Definition Of Life

Do you have a definite definition of life? Can you explain it without any confusion? Many people have different understanding about life, since everyone does not have the same life experience. We get to cope with our life by comparing it with other lives. We always wanted to be better than others. There is no reason for anyone to say why we are all competing so badly, thinking that we have some validity and prove to people around us that we are living the best life.

Great knowledge of life has been always missing from us since we never take our life very seriously or know how to live our life free from all struggles and sufferings. You never had an idea to look at this life at a very extreme level of hype, creating a lot of nuisances. Creating a greater wisdom for the life you are living is such a wonderful practice, where we are not allowed to explore at all.

Simply, there is always a pleasant suffering, when you are understanding life's reality. You need to assume that everything around you is an illusion. It is actually bound within time and space. When you get into the realisation of the beauty of life's journey, everything starts falling into place. Letting you understand the life expression which is an indefinite illusion based upon each people's manifestation.

There has always been a path for every individual born on this earth. Do we really have any idea? Always assuming that death is the end of life, but actually it is passing from this existing life and moving to higher graded life to perform better action, than this present life.

You never have to plan anything before, because nothing happens as we plan since the creator's plan is highly distinguished for everyone. The creator lets you play with your life to see how well we have disciplined our life karma. Have we taken any new chances to dissolve our karma and taken life to the next step?

Each and every cause or situation is trying to tell us that we are such a special divine being and we have to stop behaving like humans. But everything on this earth is happening vice versa, since we have nothing to prove what a powerful divine energy we are. Only an individual's special experience of higher dimension of life will make them understand, how much credibility and responsibility we have towards our life.

We are not even taking anything seriously to improve our life towards moving to the oneness of life's creation. We think, it is a waste of time and this divine path would stop us from living this materialistic and family life.

Moving to a spiritual life journey always makes everyone uncomfortable since it is not as easy as the illusion life because, for such a long period of time, you have been conditioned to this illusion life. Getting detached and understanding that the physical you are not the real you.

You're only an energy body, always trying to identify yourself and others with this physical identity. There is no mention or any respect for this physical identity you have been carrying so far, since the path of the divines only see how pure is your soul and what type of actions you have performed in this present moment.

Somehow, try to heal your life with all the difficulties which you have carried for so many lifetimes. As you heal, you are always moving one step ahead in your life's journey. As your direction and thought of life changes, you will start seeing life in every different aspect and you will get to see the reality of life at every step.

Spiritual Path: The inner journey within you, which opens up the vast universe that has been existing for a very long period of time, shows you how beautiful life has been and that it is especially designed for you.

Biochemistry Of Your Life

We are the physiological beings named as humans residing inside a flesh structure in a particular way. There is a very wide range of living beings, living along with us on this earth plane. We are always associated with the body and its structure, believing that this body is a necessity for our living on this earth. Yes, it is true that to be alive we need this body. This body is making and helping us to move from one place to another. But we are mesmerised with the beauty of our body, believing that the existence of life experience is because of the body. Since everyone assumes that this physical body is me.

As of now this physical body is giving me good health, attracting people and getting a good job. Everything in our life is an experience, depending upon our body & body structure. We think that this body is giving good and bad things in life. It is partially true because your life is not dependent on this physical body but it is dependent on the body vehicle you carry.

Is it quite confusing actually, isn't it? To survive and to live on this earth we need this body. Not only so we have to take care of this body health wise, but it's also necessary for our presence on this earth. But we are not bothered about our body's health, as we like eating and making use of this body.

We humans are very bad at using our physical body in order to experience happiness. Assuming that, keeping and feeling happiness in the body is necessary. Yes, it may be necessary but in reality - Are we behaving so? We have made our body a garbage bin by eating unwanted things, having unwanted sex, using narcotics, cosmetics, technology and so on. There is no limitation to misuse our body since we are only looking for external happiness that we may experience.

Every life existence is trying to get joy and pleasure out of this body using ecstasy that is making us feel the enjoyment. Are we not really bothered or not having time to take care of this body?

Each and every human can get enough with body, when you actually come to realise that without the purity of body you are not going to reach the path of Enlightenment.

Do understand this physical body is a vessel holding your soul it can attain enlightenment and become one with Highest Source Energy. Without your body you will not be able to dissolve your karma. Not having a body, what would you be able to do? It is really a waste. Every soul needs a body to reach its destiny. As long as you are healthy, the soul will have more lifetimes to dissolve your karma. Otherwise, this soul will not get any chance to dissolve most of your karma for this little period of time that you are living on this earth.

Living a healthy life for a large period of time gives this soul time to heal and to get better as much as possible. Understand that the body is not only you, your soul is you too. Help your soul to have a life as much as possible until it is having this body.

Being healthy brings a lot of healthy reactions in your body. Very good chemical reactions take place like functioning of your heart, good digestion, keeping your bones strong etc. Not only so, proper hormones are released at proper time to give us a good body. We can keep on counting, as there are such a lot of reactions and hormones being released at each and every moment of our life. Every chemical reaction helps us to build a healthy body. But we are not doing so; we are doing everything against our body, and that only leads to unhealthy reactions and unwanted health disasters. Whatever you feed this body, chemical reactions keep happening without our knowledge.

Most of the humans have taken everything for granted. We are not conscious and aware of what we are feeding to our mind and body, externally.

Always remember that mind, body and soul are all interconnected, when even one thing is corrupted, your life will become more miserable than you have expected and you will be suffering each and every moment of your life.

So be careful dear humans, this mind, body & soul is much more important than any other thing. Your only purpose is to dissolve your karma and get in oneness with the highest source from where you came. Hence be very careful and aware of how much you are able to take care of your health. Do not get entangled in this materialistic life which will never give you any permanent peace and happiness.

The greatest wealth of your life is only your health, not the materials around you.

Are You Doubting Yourself?

"Everything is one small realisation, that every life born on this earth is a wholesome powerful energy source which is residing within yourself as SOUL".

Never caring about anything, may feel to be like freedom from everything, but it is not so. Letting yourself to be happy and caring for others is real freedom. You don't understand this concept, since we think, we are here to get rid of everything and enjoy greater happiness without involving anyone else. Since you do behave like this, you feel free from everything and never realise what you are doing to yourself. You have always learned to handle yourself in some other different way, doubting yourself that you would not achieve or be happy until you resist everything around you. Greater knowledge is to understand that externally you might be induced with hindrance or obstacles but the greatest resistance is not from the outside of you, it is actually within you, so much that it creates doubt about yourself.

Lack of realisation and understanding of oneself always give you doubt of believing about the greater life you got. Not knowing and understanding yourself is the greatest hindrance and mistake, one can make to oneself. How can we humans be so miserable not knowing ourselves but trying to understand that everything is happening around us?

Doubting yourself is the greatest resistance of oneself, even if you try to skill up or try to learn new things, for increasing your talent etc. Whatever it might be, everything will go in vain, when one small doubt arises against you. You have nothing to do with the skills and talents you have, to know about yourself.

Only peace of mind and consciousness of life is more than enough for one to sustain this human life happily and realise what is happening within you. You have to get rid of the ability of thinking, that you are not enough. You need to stop comparing and judging yourself with other's lives. Do understand that no one is up and no one is below.

Better realise that everything is powerful as the human soul. Only your soul in this world knows how to get out of this illusion and let you live this life pleasantly.

SOUL is a mass existence, a structure less creation filled with all the sources that you require for lifetime. It is more powerful and mystical than you can imagine. It is the greatest guru, guide and path changer for your entire life. Just catch the SOUL properly and correctly, in such a way that you never need anyone's advice or help to lead this life peacefully. If you have already created a connection with your soul, do understand dear ones, you are the blessed being than anyone in this world.

Getting to know and being connected to the soul is not the easiest thing that happens to everyone's life. Only certain blessed beings get to have it in this lifetime. You are a chosen child of God, where the soul gets a chance to take you onto the path of enlightenment, to reach the oneness.

Better give up doubting yourself and stop getting feared about success and failure, which is not truly present. Throw away all the concepts of manmade rules and ideas. It does not owe you anything. All the criticism, opinions and judgements were just built to destroy humans thinking about one's own self. Society rules, regulations and lifestyle have erased everything and are not letting any humans understand themselves.

You have not come to this earth plain to live this ordinary human life. You have more than this, to do and work for it to reach the greatest source. Only you can strive to build the relationship within yourself.

Doubting is the only path to self-destruction. Don't be the quitter of your life. Let yourself live this life, at least your soul gets a chance to do, what it is meant to do in this lifetime.

Benefits Of Being Human

Wow! What a great topic to be revealed for everyone. Everything in life has a cause, similarly the life and the birth of human beings has it effects in its own way. Great assumptions and thoughts flow as you realise what type of a being, you are born on this earth.

Being a human is a blessing, if you have realised. If not, it would be very difficult to understand the life you are living on this earth. There have always been certain necessities to this life because a human nature or possessing a human nature has the greatest effect on you. You are not born simply; everything hides a particular reason for you. As the assuming and believing of life takes another shift, you will come to know why you have been born as human on this particular planet.

Every human thinks they are a particular creature, born into a life of suffering from the unknown, which is not explained by anyone. Since there exists a particular range of dimensions, that are meant and created for you to live a life of consciousness and awareness.

You never decided to be a human being nor did anyone on this earth planned to bring you to this universe. It is only this power of the Supreme Energy with unknown existence that is deciding and creating every life in this universe. We humans are powerless, to decide what type of birth to take at each lifetime. It is only decided by the **Highest Supreme Power,** who decides where and how to be born, for every life that you are born into and ultimately pass away.

There is a great importance for every life that is living on this planet but a human birth is so valuable that no one understands its power. Every birth happens depending upon your karmic results.

So, if you are born as a human you become more powerful and understand that you have moved to one extra step above in your life. You humans are always designated to know your life's secrets. Understanding the secret of life is very important for every human being, since you are led to be born on this earth for this purpose.

Since you are born on this earth your approach to life should be different from other creatures on this earth. You have to do an internal research of your life. What is the purpose of this human birth? Without any reason nothing works for you. There are lots of benefits for being born as a human being. You are always seen as one step ahead in life to reach your highest self. Reaching your highest self, is not as easy a process as you think because we assume that praying and worshipping **GOD** daily will give you its **(GOD)** presence in life. There is no connection between prayers and worshipping to reach the highest self of this universe. Everything is happening through karmic action. Being born as a human you get more benefits for dissolving your karma.

On this earth you are the only creature having your spine up, which is very much needed to get enlightened in your life. Since the erect spine helps you to pull a lot of universe power within you, bring more awareness and consciousness of self-realisation.

Only a person with awareness of the benefits of being born as human would not regret taking this human life. As you become a beneficiary, for just being born as human, you get to know how powerful and miraculous you are. Understand you are always connected with the universe and there is nothing that can separate you both. But when you become a conscious being, more cosmic energy flows into your life, creating different dimension experiences which are really needed for life expansion and get in oneness with **GOD**.

The **GOD** dimension is at a higher rate of creating power and a wonderful life for the existence of humans. You are born as a human to take blessings, as you are already in the path of wisdom and ready to reach the destination from where you came.

You are also the greatest consciousness as powerful as **GOD**. Keep on experiencing **GOD'S** power in every aspect of your life.

Respect To Yourself

Indeed, in life everyone is looking for some respect at each and every moment. Human's life is always searching for something, to keep them in a survival mode. Unawareness in life has taken human beings to a very far place, where these humans have lost all their reality and originality of understanding. These humans don't understand how far they have travelled while running on the back of this materialistic life. This materialistic life has spoiled these humans so much that they are not even aware. Why have they come to this earth with so much suffering and pain? This unconscious life has made these humans life so hectic that they believe there is no getaway.

Life has always kept you so busy that you cannot escape from anywhere. There have been so many misunderstandings in life, which are not letting you to lift your head and see what is actually happening around. You have been shaved out of the reality even without your knowledge. You are prevented from suspecting the true origin of life without even realising it.

Everything you believe is actually not real. You are mesmerised in every aspect of life, let be your relationship, money, status, job, everything is made so perfect that you cannot escape the matrix. Your belief system has got entangled within this matrix, believing strongly the unreality of life.

These unreal things are strong enough to keep us inside this illusion life, so that we are always living an unconscious life. This life has become so hard and difficult to sustain, that we live only for others sake and not able to live for happiness. This life has made us slaves to other people's happiness and requirements. It is so rigid for us that we keep on sacrificing ourselves, to show love and respect that we have for others, not knowing that we are diminishing ourselves, to keep others ignited.

Humans have to understand that every reality is hidden inside an illusion. This illusion will keep on pulling you from one place to another, for every little thing that happens only for us, so that we will understand the purpose of life. But we are afraid to see, what this life is trying to tell us. As we see more consciously and knowingly into our life, we will slowly understand that something different is happening to us, which we have forgotten to look into.

As your awareness increases, you will soon realise that something inside you is telling you that there's something you are not able to understand. As the process of understanding keeps going, you will be able to see the real inner being that is living inside you. That is none other than your **SOUL**. It is the real thing which has come to live on this earth, to finish all its karmic debts.

A sudden spark will happen to you when you realise and feel your **SOUL**, how beautiful it is. **SOUL** - It is a real thing that is holding you so strongly throughout your lifespan. Even if you give up on it, your **SOUL** will not give up on you. Do understand that your physical body has not come to live this life. It is your **SOUL'S** life to live this life there is nothing to do with yourself (physical body). Learn to keep your **SOUL'S** body always happy and respectful. Because it is made with abundance of love, compassion, prosperity and peace, where there is nothing missing in your **SOUL** system. Only you humans have built a life of want, believing this reality and always putting yourself in guilt, shame, stress, fear and depression.

But your **SOUL** carries nothing as you carry. Your **SOUL** is a wholesome and copious divine being which has come to renew the life system, with help of the physical body it holds. Your **SOUL'S** path is your life path. Nothing more or less you need not to learn externally, to make your **SOUL** achieve its oneness, with the highest source of energy.

The **SOUL** inside you knows everything in this universe. You need not help or teach your **SOUL** anything. You just listen to your **SOUL'S** inner voice and follow, even if obstacles come in your way. Because it is preparing you for the path of enlightenment and making you understand, by keeping you aware of where you came, and that where you have to return.

Letter To My Guru

"Better be with a Guru alone than staying in the company of the people who have no intention of life to live on purpose".

Hi Guru! My divine God. The way you treat me is so miraculous. Nobody can sense, how a Guru would treat a student. Does anyone have an idea? None do have, since every Guru is very special. How can a Guru be so special than anyone? Is it possible to classify them under any specialty? Maybe we could classify them under the specialty of the power they perform. But in my point of view, every Guru is very special.

Not all Gurus get connected to your soul since everybody's soul is different. As well as your Guru chooses you and decides to whom they will guide for a particular period of time. These Gurus are so adorable they are limitless and very powerful. They live life on purpose for each and every moment of their presence and either in the form of a physical and non-physical body. We always identify our Guru, to be in a physical form in the past or a living form at present. Where do these Gurus come from? Nobody knows, but when there is a search for Guru by an individual, the Guru appears in front of you either in a physical and non-physical form, at the correct time, when you are looking for guidance and want to move on the path of spirituality.

Everything in your life has a reason to happen; similarly, receiving a teaching from a Guru happens on purpose with help of your karma. The Guru always appears when a student is ready. Here, a student being ready is nothing but an individual who is ready to realise themselves. Who they are? What is the purpose of life? For which reason do they have to come to live on this earth plane?

In any part of life, we always need guidance and support from someone to take our life to the next step. Similarly, when your life is taking the direction to self-realisation, we need a person to guide us and show the path of righteousness. The Guru always tells what to do, but only we have to decide, how to do it. But the secret I learnt is that there's always a divine force (Guru) who is always pushing us to do, to get the result as needed. It is a situation, that you will realise how well your Guru handles in such a way that we think as if we are doing. Every action in life has an involvement of divine energy force. When we are properly connected to our divineness and Guru, miracles start to happen. The connection of life, between a Guru and student can go for any number of years. For some, it may be for short period and for some a long period, till the end of life.

In this world each and everything is teaching us something or the other, where everything becomes Guru for every different situation. But then comes one special divine, where it shifts your life to the next dimension, which we would not have realised.

My Guru is very sweet and always favourable, sometimes answering to my requirements immediately and sometimes not answering at all. Most of the times my

Guru leaves me to a situation, where I have to handle the real life situation. Guru is one person who trains you and put you in that part of life where you can withstand any difficult life situation. In that way, Guru can be angry, sometimes funny, often kind, and would always taking care of you.

I was always connected to my divineness, in every way and was always lucky enough to get connected to the gods, to whom all I prayed. Every and most of the superficial energy sources always stayed connected to me in their own way, and I was able to understand, sense, feel, every action and word they spoke to me. And I always believed and surrendered to my Guru, so I was always open to receive the guidance and miracles they performed for me. There are no words to explain, how well I was receiving the guidance time to time. These Gurus always made me feel so great and powerful about my birth. To be honest with everyone, I am really a blessed child of this universe receiving every guidance and support at every moment of life.

This Letter to my Guru is very special and dedicated to the guidance I have received for the past two years.

To my dearest Guru,

Guru Charanam (I surrender to the feet of my Guru). What more to tell, when there are no words to appreciate. You are my divine God who brought me into the life of spirituality. You have been so great, patient and loving, and always been there whenever I needed you. I always look for you whenever I feel down, and you are the one and the only with whom till today, I have shared all my good and bad things with you. I never missed you any single day. Always feel your presence, even though you are not in a physical form.

Your divineness is so great, that you made me realise the power hidden in me. You are the greatest protector and guidance of my life. Our relationship was a secret but more dynamically powerful, that no person could understand.

My loving Guru, everybody thinks I am the real author of this book but actually it is you, the real writer of this book. I know nobody would believe, but only I can understand how suddenly, a clueless woman like me, who had no idea about wisdom or writing skills, could transform herself into an author for such a magnificent, powerful and knowledgeable book.

Really to be open, my Guru, you made me a writer and blessed to become a specialised author of spirituality. I know that each and every word written in this book is only from your vision and ideas. It flows like a river, whenever I sit to write. You were the person who gave me consciousness and strength to write such a book of self-development.

Even now writing this letter to you is also your guidance which is flowing through me like river water, in a particular direction. Really, thank you, thank you Guru for identifying and connecting to me. Day by day, our relationship and love for each other is growing so strongly.

I, Shobhana - the blessed child of this divine universe, surrender this book to you. I behold myself and feel very great to be a tool for writing this book. I know "How powerful this book is", holding all the information on how to lead your life on self - realisation (spiritually).

As I write the letter to you, only I know how easily you made me write each and every powerful word that would become every individual's life.

Dear divineness, I am very thankful and grateful for helping me to complete my purpose. You have initiated my new life journey, as an author and I know, where I have to take it further. The purpose I hold which is given by you will be fulfilled as I serve the people around me.

Thank you, my dear Guru.

My Point Of View On My Life

Every person's life has something to share with everyone. Similarly, even my life was full of disaster, punishment, worries and problems. I never ever attempted to know why these things were always happening to me. I believed that I have been cursed to have this life. Nothing seemed to work at any part of my life. Even though I was getting a lot of help from my family and friends, nothing seemed to improve or change. Life for me always seemed to be very painful and mysterious, since nothing worked out personally and professionally.

Every hard work went in vain; nothing was going my way. I always used to think about how to prove myself to this world. In what way, I can be successful like other people but till now nothing worked. I used to think, I was always destined to live a life of uselessness, incompetence and a destroyer of happiness of my own life.

But everyone has to expect and believe that miracles always do happen in every one's life. Yes, in my life everything started changing into a blessing mode, in its own way. Everyone might think that I must have started getting good at my profession and in my personal life. Not at all, everything started happening, above all expectations.

Yes, my life started changing totally, step by step unconsciously. I was not even aware of what was happening to me. A real wanting and realisation within me started to change. Self-realisation of my life started opening up, suddenly which made me realise - Why have I taken this birth? Why am I living in this way? What is the reason to be born on this earth? A great revelation of my life's purpose, started to get realised to me with my awareness.

My life started becoming more blessed with the revelation - Why has this birth happened on this earth? Yes, I was spiritually awakened in a certain way, but even many times I was not able to understand. Slowly, day by day, month by month, it became understandable that the life, I am living is an illusion and nothing is real. I was always guided by gurus, spiritual energies and all positive energies, who were trying to push me to a different realm of life. A lot of dimensional shift started taking place. Even though I have not undergone any proper spiritual practice or received any initiation from a guru, I was always guided and supported by a lot of non-physical positive energies guiding me what I have to do and what all I have to practice.

There seemed to be great changes happening in my life which cannot be explained and shown. Even this spiritual journey, has taken me on a roller coaster. It always tries to bring wisdom to me at every moment of life. I was really astonished by, what was happening around me. But the divine source made me understand, my purpose to be on this earth.

I learnt that I have to serve people. I became more considerate towards my spiritual journey, even though there was no greater change in my life. But I was transformed personally and was living life, in a different way, that nobody had any idea.

In this way, not only my life did change, but my Guru transformed my entire way of thinking and appointed me as an author. This writer's journey was a very new chapter of my life without knowing, what to start and how to start.

Finally, a year back, I became a professional writer, where I was completely 100% guided by my Guru. Which all started like - What to write? How to write? Now also these lines that you are reading are only told and guided by my divine source.

Everything is divine, you, me and everything around us. Nothing seems to happen on its own. All the things around us are guided, planned and directed by the Higher Source energy and come to a realisation, that everything is planned beforehand. Don't take life very seriously. Everything that is meant for you will flow to you at the right time. So be happy and live this life that is flowing in front of you.

What Questions You Have, Ask Me

1. I don't know anything?

As you get into this spiritual plane or dimension, you will start realising that you don't know anything about this new life. Everything in this life has started from nothing. Similarly, this journey of spiritual life will also take you from a place you don't know. Since the life you have entered is a divine region where there are so many things that you have not realised, will come to your realisation one after the other. But in this birth, you would not be able to capture everything in this universe.

2. As you are here too? Why I am not everywhere?

Who said you are not everywhere? Your realisation has stopped only with your physical body. You think that only the physical body is you. Actually, it is not so. You are an energy body, locked up inside the physical body. Only your body can be constrained, not your energy. It travels all around the universe every second. It is a part of your imagination that you are limited. You are every form of life. Nothing is destroyed or hidden. Every energy of you has taken its own shape and form, where you are not able to identify and feel it. Only our greater consciousness will take you to the awareness that you are present in every part of this space.

3. What can be a greater understanding that the human being has to realise?

There is a lot of understanding which has to be put forth to this human life. Never regret for all the things you have realised so far. But be into an understanding that the life you live is not permanent and you cannot be real. Everything around us is surrounded by an illusion, which will disappear one after the other. You need not put any stress to live this life. It is only a game of life and death, letting you to undergo the experience of your karma. Do understand that you did not start anything, everything started from the universe. You just come to this earth to gain experience of your life.

4. Who is answering all my questions?

You already know it but you wish to get an answer from me. Right, who do you think is answering all your questions? Do you have a guess? Absolutely, I'm your SOUL GOD, acting and always a part of you. Don't individualise me as a separate being. I am you and I am the only you, answering all your questions that you need.

5. Why did you choose me to do this work (writing)?

It is not choosing you. You have already shaped yourself to be and taken for this work under your own self. You have put in a lot of hard work in your past lives. You are the blessed being, to do this work in this life. Now you are supported and guided by all the good beings, from all the divine planes trying to transcend your life into different dimensions in this lifetime. You are the doer, where you serve to be the author of this book.

6. Anything special about me to bring into this writing work?

Yes. There is a lot to say. You are meant to do this writing work in this life, which has a great purpose to serve other people's needs. It is so specialised, in a very different way from other spiritual books. You are the holder of this book. You deserve all the rights, to write this book because you have already lived the life of how a human being has to live, as mentioned in this book. It is your own life behaviour, how have you lived in your past life is now continuing and playing its roles. Very soon you will also achieve your true self. I know you are a pure soul by your thoughts and feelings, but your mind is trying to stop you from achieving what you are actually. Being the divine realised soul, you are getting into a different world which will change your life in and around you. You are very much specialised in your way, which is now doing undercover jobs. But everything on the right time will make you know, how valuable and talented you are.

7. What are our options available in our life?

There are many options to live your life happily. But is that giving you meaningful happiness and peace? Never, you humans get indulged in this materialistic life, believing that these are the best ways to live life and you have achieved success, but not so. You might think that there always exist many options to live, but for this human existence, the real option and only one option is getting in oneness with the higher source.

8. How do we get enlightened within ourselves?

Very good question! Every human should understand and realise because you are here to experience life, in order to get an awareness of the life you are living and believe that every life born on this earth has a very special purpose, this purpose has to be lived by everyone. And there arise questions of awareness in the form of **"WHO AM I"**, it is then that the first enlightenment takes place and as you flow along the direction of your soul, the real enlightenment happens.

9. Do we need great knowledge to get enlightened?

No, not necessarily. Enlightenment has nothing to do with the knowledge you possess. More information gathered makes it difficult to move into awareness of life since only the logical mind works. Enlightenment is not logical. It is a form of being full of universal wisdom, where it draws you close to the Source (GOD) easily.

10. How to emit the goodness of life?

There is nothing like good and bad in this world. It is the way you assume things and handle it in the way you understand it. Every situation or moment has both sides, positive and negative. Only the way we choose to have a situation in our life is assumed in our favour. Running behind goodness might make you forget to see other things in the world that are happening simultaneously. So don't get hung up on the goodness in life. Always try to make your life feel better than it was earlier and learn how well you have shifted your consciousness of seeing this world.

11. After the achievement what is left behind in this life?

Do you think there is something big waiting after all your achievements? Realise the reality, there is nothing left behind apart from reaching and becoming one with God. This life was formed from nothingness, after everything in this life you have to go back to nothingness of oneness named - **GOD.**

12. Have you (God) ever been tested into reality?

Why not, several times, more than humans only I have been tested in several ways, where I cannot imagine. Many people failed since I was not up to their expectations since I do not perform any small action to your willingness. All my (God) activities & blessings depend only upon your karma. Many humans live a life of doubt and fear, where God would not help or save, according to their wish. I work only upon the karmic debts.

13. Let me go, when we get into this feeling?

One and only desire to leave everything and everyone comes, when you attain eternity of life. There is a great understanding and meaning involved in it. The person who is enlightened is destined to be so, since there is an emptiness in mind that has only space for nothingness. When there is a great realisation of your nothingness of life, you will feel free to go away from where you had been held.

14. Assumption of life?

There are a lot of things in this life that are going under assumption. It exists both in the illusion and reality of life being. But the only thing is that humans greatly fail to differentiate the illusion and reality, finally fall in the lap of illusion.

15. What is the requirement to be in this life?

Everyone has a very special requirement to live this life as it flows. When you start disturbing the life flow, you get depressed and stressed. Apart from this you have come to live this life to gain special knowledge through the karma you have performed in the past. As well as you are here to gain experience, which will take you to the next level of life, where you will get knowledge to take life onto the path of enlightenment.

16. Have I gained enough knowledge to live this life?

No not at all. No human gains enough knowledge to survive on this earth. This life is a learning process so there is nothing like you have learned everything. You are always on the track of learning, as well as you have come here to gain wisdom, which will give you liberation from this worldly life.

17. What have I learnt so far?

Nothing, it is so simple. Life starts from nothing and ends with nothing. There is nothing to learn only realisation of what is happening to you is more than enough for you to experience this life. Don't come to conclusion because there is no beginning and end in this life that matters. Everything is only in existence. Don't learn, realise the being.

18. What is my current reality?

Your life is full of rash realities of disaster. There is nothing to blame you, since everyone is living a life of disaster and that too unknowingly. Lack of consciousness and awareness of humans are engulfing disaster in every possible way. You being one of the ways, you also have to go through the same situation. Try to save yourself and others at the earliest. There is very little time to get out of this illusioned life.

19. What life is mystical?

Everybody's life is mystical. You think everything is actually working logically and there is no interference of life force. What you see and think is nothing related to your actions but it looks like it is happening only because of your actions. Actually, it is not so. Everything happening in this universe is mystical, which matches your actions. Everything seems to be logical but actually everything works beyond illogical forces.

20. Who cares for him or her (GOD force)?

Nobody cares, since God force is unknown, actually unseen and seamlessly nothing, which is trying to keep this life system in the universe bonded together. This God force or an entity in the form of energy is trying to keep every single matter in alignment with its own energy. So, whatever you want in the universe, cannot escape from God's force. And this force does not need any one to take care of it.

21. What source of energy is required for inner development?

You are the source of energy and it already exists within you. You only need to trigger that energy. The life force (inner energy) will do all those things that are required for your inner self development. Just learn to understand and identify your source energy at the earliest. In order to achieve the purpose of life you are meant to live.

22. What God knows about you?

GOD knows everything about you. GOD is the wholesome creator of this universe, which exists in the highest form of energy. Only this energy knows - Who you are? Where are you? Why are you here? Only God knows this complete creation and its purpose. Not even a single energy entity of different forms has recognized and understood the real formation of this life being. GOD - the unknown being in an extravagant form with strong energy force.

23. Which is the best creation or the creator?

Obviously, the creator is the best. Without this wonderful creator these beautiful creations would not be available to us.

24. Is the divine power, the real power?

Actually, not divine power. You only have different names. We all are naturally powerful but it is hidden within us, only when triggered with certain powerful sources, your real power comes out. You can name this power as divine power or spiritual power but you are the real power, only the name changes. You don't feel the power because everything is powerful in its own existence.

Conclusion

Here comes the great conclusion of this book. A life book that is expected to change millions and millions of lives. You will be cherished by each chapter as you read where it will put you into a different perspective of life. It is sure to bring a lot of awareness and consciousness about life.

This book not only reveals how a human being has to live on this earth but also showers light in various life stages on how important this life is. It really will give you a clear picture of life that you have lived so far. Any normal human being can understand what type of miserable life, they have lived and what all trolls this karma has taken up on their life.

Here you will get into a lot of realisations, how easy life is to live. But we physical beings have made it so complicated by running behind these materialistic things and have lost the knowledge and wisdom to understand, why we are here. Still now many are not even ready to understand and realise the purpose of life. Each and every being on this earth is meant to live this life for a particular purpose.

You are not meant to live a generalised life, you are a special divine source born here to perform a particular action that shifts your dimension and removes all the blocks that are hindering you, from achieving the real source of energy. So, as early as possible, try to bring a chance to know about yourself - What you are?

This book has given me a great chance to reveal my soul identity - What I had been earlier and what is the purpose of life to live here? As it opens to the reality of life, which I have not imagined and not even realised. This book is a great mystery of life for me, which has revealed every stage of life that I have to live.

A great opportunity is always presented in front of you in different forms. But grab at the earliest and come to a realisation of your purpose. Live a life of love and compassion, become a source of help for the people who really need you.

You are the enchanted being, blessed to achieve all the needful things to attain your purpose. The real source is waiting to join its hands with you.

Be The Change And Bring Change Around You.

www.ingramcontent.com/pod-product-compliance
Lightning Source LLC
LaVergne TN
LVHW061540070526
838199LV00077B/6845